T0309175

ROUTLEDGE LIBRARY EDITIONS: MANAGEMENT

Volume 24

THE PHOTOFIT MANAGER

THE PHOTOFIT MANAGER

Building a picture of management in the 1990s

Edited by
MARION DEVINE

Routledge
Taylor & Francis Group

LONDON AND NEW YORK

First published in 1990 by Unwin Hyman Ltd

This edition first published in 2018
by Routledge
2 Park Square, Milton Park, Abingdon, Oxon OX14 4RN

and by Routledge
711 Third Avenue, New York, NY 10017

Routledge is an imprint of the Taylor & Francis Group, an informa business

British Library Cataloguing in Publication Data
A catalogue record for this book is available from the British Library

ISBN: 978-1-138-55938-7 (Set)
ISBN: 978-1-351-05538-3 (Set) (ebk)
ISBN: 978-0-8153-5551-9 (Volume 24) (hbk)
ISBN: 978-1-351-12956-5 (Volume 24) (ebk)

Publisher's Note
The publisher has gone to great lengths to ensure the quality of this reprint but points out that some imperfections in the original copies may be apparent.

Disclaimer
The publisher has made every effort to trace copyright holders and would welcome correspondence from those they have been unable to trace.

The Photofit Manager

Building a picture of management in the 1990s

Edited by
MARION DEVINE

London
UNWIN HYMAN

Published by the Academic Division of
Unwin Hyman Ltd
15/17 Broadwick Street, London W1V 1FP, UK

Unwin Hyman, Inc.
8 Winchester Place, Winchester, Mass. 01890, USA

Allen & Unwin (Australia) Ltd,
8 Napier Street, North Sydney, NSW 2060, Australia

Allen & Unwin (New Zealand) Ltd in association with the
Port Nicholson Press Ltd
Compusales Building, 75 Ghuznee Street, Wellington 1, New Zealand

First published in 1990

British Library Cataloguing in Publication Data
The photofit manager.
1. Business firms. Managers. training & development
I. Devine, Marion, *1963*–
658.4'07124

ISBN 0–04–440505–7

Library of Congress Cataloging in Publication Data
The Photofit manager : building a picture of management in the 1990s /
edited by Marion Devine.
p. cm.
Includes bibliographical references.
ISBN 0–04–440505–7
1. Executive ability. 2. Performance. I. Devine, Marion.
HD38. 2.P49   1990
658.4'09—dc20   89–38775
                                                           CIP

Typeset in 11 on 13 point Garamond
Printed and bound in Great Britain by
Hartnolls Ltd, Bodmin, Cornwall

Contents

Notes on contributors

Stephen Bevan is a graduate of Aston University Management Centre and worked initially in the research unit of Ashridge Management College. Since joining the IMS in 1982, he has conducted research and consultancy studies in the areas of skill definition and development and retention of key staff. In recent years his work has focused on career and development issues for graduates and managerial staff. Publications include: *The management of labour turnover* 1988 (with Wendy Hirsh), IMS Report 144; and *Employee selection in the UK* (with Julie Fryatt), IMS Report 161.

Dr Tom Boydell is director of the consultancy Transform. After graduating as a mechanical engineer, he worked in aircraft components. He then moved to the fields of management learning and development, first at Sheffield Polytechnic and then with Transform. His doctoral research was into client-centred learning and how to measure its effects. He has written some 12 books on aspects of management development. He is currently working with major multi-national and nationalized industries on the developmental aspects of total quality.

Wendy Briner is Director of Ashridge Teamworking Services. After graduating with a degree in economics she successfully completed a Certificate in Education and an MSC in administrative sciences from the City Graduate Business Centre. Wendy taught personnel management and industrial training at Middlesex Polytechnic. She then spent one year at the College of Europe in Bruges studying the social and economic policies of the European Communities. From 1978 she spent several years working for Hewlett-Packard both in the UK and in Europe as an internal consultant and trainer. More recently she worked as an external consultant. She joined Ashridge in September 1986.

Christopher Bull is the Principal of Christopher Bull Associates, a network of organization development consultants and trainers. He has worked in the field of personal, social and organization development for the past 16 years and currently works with a number of national and multi-national commercial enterprises and public sector organizations. His interests are in developing and applying concepts and practical approaches that enable people to identify and fulfil their potential both as individuals and as members of varying organizational forms.

Professor John Burgoyne is a founder member of the Department of Management Learning in the School of Management, Lancaster University. After graduating in psychology and working briefly in applied psychology he entered the growing field of management education in 1968 as a research fellow at Manchester Business School, where he later became a lecturer. In 1974 he went to Lancaster University as a founder member of the Centre for the Study of Management Learning. He is currently working on the launch of part-time MBA and Diploma programmes in collaboration with industry and work organizations.

Marion Devine is a management journalist and writer. She has a regular column with the *Sunday Times* and frequently contributes to a number of publications including *The Times* and *The Director*. She is a senior researcher with Ashridge, where she acts as a consultant on a range of editorial and research projects. Her publications include *Everyone needs a mentor, Clore: the man and his millions, Management buyouts* and *Businesswoman*.

Dr Charles Dodd works for Cambridgeshire County Council as the Assistant Director for management and organizational development. He read classics and then English at Oxford University and he has a higher degree for research into organizational change. After service with the Royal Air Force in a range of teaching and administrative posts in the UK and Cyprus, he worked in management development in further and higher education before joining Cambridgeshire. He is qualified in psychometric testing and he has published work on staff development, teachers' preferences for in-service education and two volumes of translations of modern Greek poetry.

Julian Greatrex now works as an independent consultant in individual and organization development. Prior to that he worked for BP International as a human resource consultant focusing particularly on assessment and development, with a strong emphasis on self development and career development and the competencies required for future effective managerial performance.

Dr Robin Jacobs is an independent research consultant. Formally a senior researcher with the Ashridge Management Research Group, he particularly focuses on the problems involved in developing valid and meaningful data about the performance of senior managers and the need to develop better, non-threatening processes for providing managers with helpful individual feedback. He recently edited the Ashridge publication *Assessing Management Competencies*, a report based on original research conducted at Ashridge that evaluated competency based assessment methods throughout the UK.

Ronnie Lessem is a Reader in International Management at City University Business School and programme manager for the new consortium MBA. He was born in Zimbabwe where he completed his first degree in economics. He acquired an MSc (Econ) from LSE and an MBA from Harvard, before gaining a PhD in business development from City University. Dr Lessem is the author of six books on management – *Enterprise development, Intrapreneurship, Heroic management, Global business, Global management principles*, and *Managing cultural change* (forthcoming). He is an editor with Basil Blackwells for a series on development management.

Eric Mitchell is a management consultant and trainer specializing in the development of organizations, managers and staff. His recent work has been concerned with personal development programmes for managers; helping managers prepare and adjust to the future privatization of an Electricity Board; the structure, resources and management in a museum. Eric is a distance learning tutor to the MBA programmes at Warwick and Henley and Academic Tutor to the consortium MBA at the City University. He is an associate of Quarto, an independent group of management consultants and trainers.

Dr Brian O'Neill is a chartered occupational psychologist and Director of Innovation Management Consultants. He provides services in management assessment and development, leadership and innovation to various organizations. After receiving a PhD in psychology and lecturing at the University of Western Ontario, he joined the business community where he has held a number of senior appointments in the UK and Canada. Before launching his own consulting business and while head of Assessment Services at British Airways, he managed the Topflight assessment programme for senior managers.

Michael Osbaldeston is Chief Executive of Ashridge Management College with overall responsibility for the College's strategic planning and co-ordinating the academic work of the three post-experience teaching groups and the MBA team, together with their supporting learning resources and hotel services. After graduating from Liverpool University with an Honours degree in biochemistry, Michael later specialized in the behavioural sciences when he took his Master of Business Administration degree. As a researcher with a firm of economic consultants, he contributed to a number of government sponsored industrial enquiries.

Peter Phillips is Manager of Human Resources at BP International. He has extensive experience of human resource consultancy, particularly on an international basis. He is currently focusing on assessment and development, with a particular emphasis on corporate high flyers.

Dr Valerie Stewart is an industrial psychologist and management writer with more than 17 years experience in helping organizations identify management potential and manage change. Author of eight best selling books on these and related subjects, she has an international consulting practice in Europe, Australia, New Zealand and South Africa. In 1988 Dr Stewart joined the Mosaic Management Consulting Group in Bristol to develop a series of programmes and processes. These have enabled widespread and effective client access to her practical approach and methodologies for the identification and development of management potential.

Ben Thompson-McCausland is Managing Director of the National
& Provincial Building Society. Before that he was Chief Executive
of the London Life Association and earlier Deputy Chairman at
Arbuthnot Latham & Co. Ltd, the merchant bank. He was educated
at Eton and Trinity College, Cambridge, where he gained a degree
in economics and history and worked for Coopers & Lybrand where
he qualified as a Chartered Accountant.

Frank Tyrrell is an independent consultant. After studying languages and philosophy at Newcastle University, he qualified as a
scientific and technical translator specializing in atomic and nuclear
physics. In 1973 he joined the management and training unit of the
Civil Aviation Authority. He also became a visiting tutor to several
other organizations. He moved to ICL as a management training
consultant where he worked with Peter Honey and developed a
more behavioural approach to interpersonal skills training. In 1981
Frank joined GEC's training and consultancy business at Dunchurch.
In 1982 he became General Manager of Dunchurch. He entered
freelance employment in 1984.

Foreword

This book is based on the extensive work which is taking place to prepare managers to cross the threshold of a new decade. Industry and education are currently grappling with the problem of how to help managers to adjust to the changing features of this era, which include new organizational structures, demographic changes and a fresh definition of internationalization.

The quest to improve managerial performance, both now and in the future, has led to considerable work on defining and developing management competences. This book examines some of these initiatives and highlights the tremendous innovative thought and creative energy that is being applied to the development of tomorrow's managers.

Companies are indeed showing that they can build pictures of the people who match their needs. The challenge to those engaged in management development is to work with businesses to create a new generation of managers – people with appropriate skills, abilities and, above all, a willingness to engage in self-motivated, life-long learning.

This book supplies practical examples of the ways in which this challenge is being met by successful organizations in the public and private sectors. It builds on the work presented at a conference organized by the Association of Management Education and Development (AMED) and Ashridge Management Research Group (*Management Profiles for the 1990s*, 4–5 January 1989). It offers stimulating ideas for those who are involved in management development, whether they are specialists or, as is increasingly the case, line managers who are responsible for their own and their staff's development.

The Photofit Manager is both a snapshot in time and part of a moving picture of management's advance into the 1990s.

Valerie Hammond
Director of Ashridge Management Research Group

Introduction:
Setting the scene

MARION DEVINE & MICHAEL OSBALDESTON

> In developing managerial competency, we must do more than 'drive through the rearview mirror'. It is not enough to look at what excellent organizations and managers are already doing. It is also necessary to be proactive in relation to the future: to anticipate some of the changes that are likely to occur and to position organizations and their members to address these new challenges effectively.
>
> Gareth Morgan, *Riding the waves of change*
> (San Francisco: Jossey-Bass)

All across Europe, organizations in industry and education are seeking more reliable ways of identifying and developing the 'competent manager'. Although these organizations vary in size and activity, they share one thing in common – a strong belief in the strategic importance of human knowledge. They recognize that their long-term competitiveness depends on their ability to develop fully and utilize the expertise and talent of all their members. Many are evolving into knowledge-based organizations whose major asset is technical know-how. To lose or ignore this know-how would be a serious, even disastrous, mistake.

Other factors have thrown the importance of the quality of management performance into high relief. A key trend is that organizational structures are becoming more diverse and complex. Many businesses are moving towards flatter, decentralized structures in order to become more fluid and market driven. This has led to a growing emphasis on 'horizontal' management,

1

which operates primarily through lateral rather than hierarchical relationships. These changes have forced businesses increasingly to depend on people, not processes.

The internationalization of markets is also causing businesses to review the type of managers they need. Many are looking for individuals who are capable of enabling people of different cultures to work effectively together. Often, the key to achieving this lies in the manager's ability to combine an in-depth understanding of his or her cultural underpinnings with an openness to other cultures. In addition, international managers need to act locally, but think and plan strategically and globally.

All these trends are making new and more onerous demands on managers. More and more, effective performance involves learning to handle complexity, diversity and ambiguity. A survey of ten top leading European companies conducted by Ashridge, a British business school, reveals that managers will need to become 'sensors', 'integrators' and 'animateurs'. Sensors are managers with a sensitive understanding of how the external environment influences an organization. Integrators are managers who manage a diverse range of lateral relationships, often from bases of influence that do not depend on a formal position. Animateurs are managers who mobilize and channel human energy.

The need to respond to all these changes has forced businesses to redefine top performance. Effectively, management is under the microscope. Specialists from the business and education sectors are now working together to dissect the management process in order to identify its most basic constituents.

This process has thrown new light on the anatomy of competency. In addition to technical and theoretical knowledge, it is now widely understood that competency includes skills, behaviours, values and even personality traits.

However, defining these generic groupings is probably the simplest task. A far more difficult challenge is to find accurate methods of assessing the specific attributes of each grouping. Once this is achieved, organizations must discover the best ways of matching the skills and behaviours of their employees with these ideal profiles. They must then consider how to tie in other systems, such as assessment, leadership succession, training and development, in order to make competency a strategic tool.

As yet, no definitive competency approach exists. One reason for this is that the concept is still relatively young. Another, more positive reason is that organizations recognize that they must develop approaches that fit their own unique business needs, workforces, corporate and national cultures. Indeed, some businesses are very anxious to keep quiet about their competency systems as they assert that they give them a vital edge over their competitors.

As a consequence, a rich array of competency methods now exist all over Europe. These vary hugely in nature. For example, in Canada Gareth Morgan is developing the concept of 'fracture forums' as a way of 'developing competences for a turbulent world'. Fracture forums aim to help managers to identify technological, social and economic developments that may reshape an industry or business and demand a new constellation of competences. He believes that a key competence is the ability to 'read' what is happening in the world and identify 'pivotal changes'. Management teams must develop skills and mindsets that enable them to recognize key events and trends, 'tune into the future' and 'engage in perception gathering twenty-four hours a day'.

In Sweden, much attention has been drawn to the importance of the individual's understanding of his or her role and task. For example, research by the University of Gothenburg into competency profiles at the Volvo Data company reveals that 'the most fundamental aspect of human competence is the individual's conception of the task'. The university discovered that the effectiveness of the company's internal mathematics and statistics consultants was determined by how they understood the nature of their tasks. Those who were most effective believed their role was actively to seek out problems to solve and to identify these problems by building up relationships with departments. In contrast, the less competent consultants believed that the customer should identify a problem, then ask for help. Only then did these consultants establish a relationship with the department. Through identifying this difference, Volvo was able to identify the competences they wanted all their technical consultants to possess and to help each one of them to question and realign their understanding of their job content.

In Denmark, Copenhagen Business School is researching into the role of 'tacit' knowledge. Through examining the managerial problems on building sites in Denmark, it discovered two parallel forms of knowledge – formal instruction and tacit, intuitive, commonsense knowledge. In some situations, these different sources of knowledge were in conflict, causing time-consuming and needless errors.

However, contrary to expectation, the research team found that formal instruction was not always a more reliable source of knowledge. In certain situations, particularly where there was 'information overload', intuition and commonsense enabled tasks to be done more speedily and efficiently. This has led Copenhagen Business School to advocate that businesses 'strike a strategic balance' between the two forms of knowledge. They should stop thinking of knowledge as 'an almost tangible, formalized fund of indisputable "truths"' and learn to recognize situations where one source of knowledge is particularly appropriate.

In Finland, the Helsinki-based Swedish School of Economics and Business Administration is exploring how individual competence can be transformed into organizational competence. It is exploring ways of 'collectivizing' to various degrees different aspects of individual competence, such as theoretical and practical knowledge; internal and external networks; methods of comprehending and organizing tasks. Through doing this, organizations can reduce their dependence on key individuals and prevent the power games that are so often played.

In the Netherlands, the Netherlands School of Business has created a 'curriculum blue print' for its business courses which is based on competences. The curriculum covers three facets: functional subject areas such as marketing and operations management; general skills, such as problem solving and effective communication; and learning skills, which help managers to 'learn to learn' and to continuously monitor, plan and adjust their behaviour and skills.

In Britain, the competency debate has gained dramatic momentum under the 'Management Charter Initiative', a powerful national movement to improve management development and training. Many major international companies, professional associations and business schools are currently engaged in a heated debate about the merit of a national system of qualifications which would be based on specific lists of competences. The proposed plan is that managers would have to demonstrate competence in a range of areas in order to progress through a three-tiered qualification system. Line managers could gain a business certificate, middle managers a business diploma and senior managers a Master of Business Administration (MBA). All these courses would have credit ratings to enable managers to work towards the qualifications as and when they were able. Also, a national credit transfer system would enable employers to design in-house training that would count towards the qualifications.

If British educational institutions wish to offer these qualifications, they will have to design their courses around the national competency framework and gain accreditation from a single, specially created, centralized body. This organization would also be responsible for determining and maintaining standards. In addition, it is proposed that a network of consortia, consisting of representatives from industry and education, would be responsible for implementing the competency framework at a local level. Lastly, assessment agencies would be formed to assess managers' performance, using methods agreed by the central organization. Already, government bodies such as the Training Agency and the Department of Trade and Industry have donated around £1.5 million to help develop the proposal.

The result of this ambitious initiative is to throw the thorny issues surrounding the competency approach into sharp relief in Britain. The competency approach is being examined from every angle, in terms of not only how to implement such a concept but even whether it has any lasting value or relevance.

Conclusion

Whatever the outcome of the current debate about competences, there is no doubt that it has given a new energy and direction to management development and human resources. Unresolved issues and dilemmas abound; disagreements about the nature and use of attributes wax fiercely. Many of these conflicting viewpoints are represented in the following chapters of this book. But no matter how these are resolved, it is clear that the journey towards competence is as important, if not more so, as the eventual destination.

The broad brushstroke: identifying effective performance

Introduction

Is there a shared language between and within organizations that describes effective performance? Are selection and assessment systems based on this common understanding? Are management development strategies built around scientifically defined core skills and behaviours?

According to Stephen Bevan (Chapter 1), the answer is no. Many organizations have only vague, subjective notions of essential managerial attributes. Plainly, a more objective method of description must replace the near guesswork that currently exists.

Bevan's assertions stem from extensive research conducted by the UK's Institute of Manpower Studies (IMS) among more than 40 employers. These organizations identified over 1,800 descriptions of key managerial skills. These descriptions were condensed into 16 common attributes. Did these represent, asked the IMS, a core curriculum for management development?

Further work revealed that this was not the case. The meaning of these attributes plainly varied within and between organizations. Now, the IMS is exploring behaviourally based rating systems, which appear to yield more reliable results. Other examples of sound methods of measurement exist within industry. However, if progress is to be made into the next decade, more organizations need to be encouraged to embrace these practices.

Although John Burgoyne (Chapter 2) supports the basic concept of competences, he departs from Bevan's viewpoint by arguing that it does not necessarily follow that performance should be broken down into specific lists of attributes. Before organizations can use competences as a basis for assessment and development, they need to address eight fundamental issues. These include whether performance can be accurately represented in fragmented lists; whether these are inevitably too general; how these lists can accommodate diversity and individuality; and how individual competency relates to the collective competence of a group or organization.

Burgoyne concludes that universal, mechanistic lists of skills and behaviours have limited value and that organizations need to adopt more flexible and holistic approaches to competency.

Robin Jacobs (Chapter 3) shares many of Burgoyne's reservations about competences but goes further in his criticisms. Drawing from a survey of 100 large organizations, he identifies a continuum of approaches to competences. While structured organizations operating in relatively stable environments value competences, a small number of devolved businesses in turbulent environments are increasingly dissatisfied with using one single definition of performance. They are looking for alternative methods that identify intangible qualities such as creativity and sensitivity.

On the basis that managerial life is becoming ever more complex and ambiguous, Jacobs argues that competences over-simplify reality and present only a partial picture of effectiveness. Organizations need to accept that performance is influenced by 'idiosyncratic' factors such as personal beliefs, aims and perceived meanings. Alternative methods, particularly self-assessment, must be considered.

Like Burgoyne and Jacobs, Tom Boydell (Chapter 4) seeks a holistic approach to competency – one that weds intangible qualities with more discernible and measurable attributes. Moving into philosophical territory, Boydell presents a model of competences that integrates the tangible with the intangible and the spiritual with the material. He identifies three strands of competences that underpin almost all managerial skills and behaviours. *Managerial attributes* include qualities such as empowering people and focusing purpose. *Modes of managing* include the ability to adapt and experiment. *Personal qualities* include stability, control and sensitivity. These three strands of competence interconnect with each other and flow constantly between the inner and outer worlds.

In the final chapter of section 1, Charles Dodd addresses the issue of how to define and assess individual competency in a collective context. He looks at how psychometric tests can enable competence to be viewed in a different light: instead of measuring individual managers against an ideal set of attributes, why not identify their strengths and weaknesses and the most appropriate roles they adopt in teams. That way, businesses build on talents and skills that already exist in the organization. In particular, Dodd advocates the use of self-assessment questionnaires, a provision that is often lacking in the competency approach. However, this exercise needs to be balanced with the perspectives of colleagues and subordinates in order to develop a full picture of individual performance. Similarly, these exercises can be used to identify the effectiveness of teams and the way individual members interact with one another.

CHAPTER 1

What makes a manager?

STEPHEN BEVAN

Amid all the rhetoric about the challenges of the 1990s, the changes to the way Europe runs its business, the effects of the demographic downturn and the changing nature of employment structures, the one thing that we can all be certain of is that our passage to the end of the century must be managed with considerable deftness. It is Europe's managers who will bear the brunt of the struggle ahead. It is they who will be held accountable for any lost business opportunities.

Some may argue that to resurrect the debate about the quality of management is something of a futile and eleventh hour gesture. Yet the question of quality is one that must be tackled urgently as it is here that most confusion exists among employers. The current debate presents businesses with many practical conflicts and choices. What, for example, is meant by the notion of managerial 'competence'? How should companies manage the careers of managers and assess their performance? How can more scientific and reliable approaches to management development replace the near guesswork that prevails in some quarters of industry?

The Institute of Manpower Studies (IMS) commonly hears employers ask a number of fundamental questions about how to utilize and develop managers. Some of the questions include the following:

• *What makes a good manager in our business?*
  Employers are still seeking an accessible and relevant way of describing the managerial attributes that are crucial to effective performance. They are also keen to know how they

can develop a successful formula of attributes to remedy current deficiencies.

- *How do we ensure that we have enough good managers for the 1990s?*
  This raises both *qualitative* and *quantitative* issues, alongside questions relating to the use of internal or external recruits and the adequacy of current succession management practices.
- *How should we use graduates to meet our requirements?*
  Should all managers in the 1990s be graduates and are 'fast-track' or 'high-flyer' schemes the most appropriate mechanisms for developing them?
- *What are the best career paths for our managers?*
  The notion of 'career posts' is often discussed, as is the way that senior positions in many organizations seem to be occupied by people in the same professions (e.g. actuaries and accountants in insurance companies). Few employers are clear about the implications of these practices.
- *What should be the balance between formal training and self-development?*
  In many companies the process of management development is dominated by formal methods of instruction (short courses, professional exams, etc.) instead of mechanisms that encourage self-development. Many wish to encourage self-development, but are unclear about how this should be managed.
- *How do we manage the careers of professional and technical staff?*
  Many organizations reward their best specialist staff by placing them in managerial posts that they are neither suited to nor want. Yet the problem of how to reward and retain them remains.

Questions such as these must be discussed against the background of the current debate about the future of management education and recent research conducted at IMS. Three central themes need to be addressed. The first issue is that of definition: what *does* make a manager? The second is that of recognition: how do we assess managerial performance and competence? The third issue focuses on the mechanisms we use to manage the careers of managers and whether these practices will remain unchallenged into the next decade.

What makes a manager?

To develop managers we have to understand *what* they do and *why* some do it so well. To gain such an understanding, we have to establish a way of talking about managerial attributes and competences that makes clear *precisely* which aspects of performance are valued. All employers have such a 'language', though they exist in a variety of forms. In order to gain a clearer picture of the languages used by large companies to describe managerial competence, IMS decided to research into the content of the language itself (Hirsh and Bevan, 1988). We were also interested to discover how firms derive their descriptions of managers, how these descriptions are used and whether it is possible to isolate good practice.

We began by approaching the corporate members of IMS and other large companies that we knew had an interest in this area. We asked them to send us any documentation they had that contained descriptions of managerial attributes, skills and competences. These were typically papers relating to managerial selection, performance appraisal, potential assessment and promotion. More than 40 employers sent us a total of over 100 forms. We analysed the content of these documents in some detail and found over 1,800 *separate* skill descriptions and, resisting any temptation to reinterpret their meaning, listed them in terms of their numerical raw frequency. Table 1.1 represents the 16 most commonly occurring words.

A number of companies used terms that relate to the manager's role as a decision-maker, communicator and leader, as well as planner and organizer. Clearly, most of the criteria against which

Table 1.1 The most common managerial attributes

* oral communication	* professional/technical skills
* leadership	* planning
* judgement	* innovation
* initiative	* appearance
* organizing	* interpersonal skills
* communication (general)	* experience
* motivation	* numeracy
* analytical skills	* maturity

Source: IMS Survey, 1988.

managers are assessed fall into these broadly similar categories and, although we found some variation between both assessment method and industrial sector, few of the attributes caused us to raise our eyebrows. Isn't this, we asked, a reassuring fact? If the same list of attributes is applicable to managers in most of the biggest and most successful companies, had we not uncovered a 'core' curriculum for management development?

The answer, of course, was 'no' because we also discovered that these common words more often than not meant very different things. Indeed, we found wide differences in interpretation both *between* organizations and *within* them. For example, in one function of a large UK company we visited, good 'decision-making' was described to us as 'making a decision only when you are in full possession of all the facts'. In another part of the same organization, the kind of 'decision-making' that was valued involved 'making a timely and perhaps calculatedly risky decision within the context of prevailing business conditions'. Both are examples of decision-making behaviour, but each represents a different and legitimate definition.

This raises the issue of assessment: if so many definitions exist, how can we give more precise and helpful guidance about criteria to those who assess managers? Unless people in organizations have a *shared understanding* of the attributes that are valued and rewarded, we have little hope of developing managers in a coordinated and meaningful way into the 1990s. But how can this shared understanding be achieved? How can we ensure that the assessment of managers and the language we use to describe aspects of their performance are based on a sufficiently detailed, scientific and yet accessible set of criteria? This has been the subject of subsequent case study work conducted by IMS.

Assessing managerial performance

During our research looking at managerial skill 'languages', one of the factors we were keen to investigate was the origin and source of the attributes that managers were measured against. For the most part, we found that subjective methods were still being used by over half the organizations we contacted. For example, we found that the selection or appraisal criteria used for managers and potential managers were often drawn up by senior managers or personnel staff, who compiled a list of attributes that they believed to be relevant. These lists were rarely based on any scientific analyses of managerial competence or on the skill requirements of managerial jobs. Instead, they were founded upon intuitive judgements of 'ideal' attributes most likely to be associated with 'good' management.

If the personnel function is the dominant source of such lists (as was the case with almost half the companies that submitted material) there is a clear need for the meaning of the attributes to be communicated to company assessors. If this is not done, two problems arise. The first is that the attributes are not based on a scientific analysis of job requirements. The second is that these inaccurate descriptions are applied inconsistently within the organization. These lead to, at best, a piecemeal approach to career management.

What is needed is a more robust and accurate way of describing managerial competence. This should not only reflect more accurately the skill, competence and behaviour required of managers in businesses, but also provide descriptions that are universally understood in assessment processes. Some companies have already taken substantial steps towards the development of such methods by developing rating scales for managerial performance which are 'behaviourally anchored'. IMS has also conducted work with such rating scales within companies and it believes that the process of deriving, developing and using them can be beneficial in several ways.

Behaviour and competences

Our approach is to use Repertory Grid and Critical Incident interviewing techniques to arrive at statements of behaviours (or outputs) that describe key aspects of managerial behaviour as demonstrated by excellent and poor performers. While these approaches are by no means new, they consistently result in a fresh view of managerial competence whenever they are used. The key to their success is the way they articulate aspects of performance that are often taken for granted or are unspoken about, yet that play an essential part in determining the difference between success and mediocrity. Table 1.2 provides some simple examples of these 'output statements' for managing staff, which illustrate their potential for use in assessment.

These statements, along with many others derived within one organization, contribute strongly to an assessment system that does not need to rely on broad headings such as 'people management', which can be widely interpreted and inconsistently applied. Another key advantage of them is that, through reducing the scope for interpretation, they become an efficient way to communicate the attributes that the organization values and rewards.

Table 1.2 Output statements: people management

EFFECTIVE	INEFFECTIVE
* Gives appropriate level of praise at the right time	* Finds fault rather than gives praise
* Generates enthusiasm in subordinates	* Can't get staff to work for him/her
* Delegates appropriately, making staff feel they have control over work	* Interferes in things that are the tasks of others

However, at this point it is necessary to sound a word of warning. Such statements of behaviour, particularly those that are derived by examining the effectiveness of good performers, occasionally throw up some interesting cultural anomalies that require interpretation before they are used for assessment. The next example of an output statement, seen in Table 1.3, illustrates this point well. It is taken from a range of statements derived from interviewing managers and indicates the qualities needed to demonstrate 'political awareness'.

Table 1.3 Output statements: political awareness

EFFECTIVE	INEFFECTIVE
* Has a wide range of company contacts and uses them to his or her own advantage	* Is parochial in outlook
* Is careful to demonstrate abilities to those with influence	* Will not stand up, shout and be noticed

In this example of political awareness we see that good managers in the company tend to display characteristics that might be described as devious and manipulative! The question the company has to ask itself is 'How explicit do we want to be about the behaviour we reward and value?' Even if this sort of behaviour is exhibited by successful managers, a decision is needed on how publicly it is to be encouraged in others. Another question might be, 'Which of these attributes should we be training managers to perform?' Some attributes will be learnable while others may be felt to be almost genetically determined. Few companies have a 'Devious and Manipulative' module on their management development programmes!

Once such editing and debate of this kind has been conducted, IMS finds that the use of these methods provides a more reliable and acceptable approach to managing the careers of managers in many organizations. However, having a more scientific and comprehensive assessment language is only the first part of the battle that needs to be fought against the 'conventional wisdom' based on guesswork. If management development is to make strides in the 1990s, it must also be based on management systems that are both sensible and appropriate. This raises the question of whether the currently fashionable ways of managing careers in organizations have any long-term value.

Career management systems

Career management practices in organizations are as much subject to fashions and trends as any other aspects of personnel practice. Our experiences with companies at IMS suggest that most of these trends begin with sound and solid good practices established by a small but pioneering group of companies (often independently of each other). However, fashion soon determines that other organizations begin to embrace them, often without the same thought or rigour as those that initiated them. This leads, in many cases, to examples of systems being used because they are thought to be, rather than *known* to be, beneficial. One example of these fashions is discussed here: 'high-flyer' or 'fast-track' schemes.

High-flyer schemes

It is common for young trainee or potential managers (increasingly graduates) to be placed on some kind of an accelerated training and development programme, which is intended to groom the select few into the company's future senior management. An important point to make about such schemes is that access to them should be based on a solid and scientifically based view of the characteristics required in senior management jobs. Second, in some organizations, they appear to be based on a sometimes fragile set of assumptions:

- Potential is something that *can* be spotted early on in a graduate's career.
- The potential of the high-flyer will still be relevant when she/he is called upon to exercise it.
- Getting to the top at a relatively early age is good for business.
- Career movement can be planned *and* achieved without interruption.
- High-flyers are willing participants in the game (if they are told they are in it).

As demand for graduates increases beyond the projected supply, and as large employers increasingly look to graduates to equip them with management material, it is likely that the high-flyer scheme will be considered by many more. Unless the numerous side-effects of such an approach are anticipated, however, the expensive lengths to which many employers go in order to recruit and develop graduates might backfire. These side-effects include:

- success becoming self-fulfilling – if high-flyers are constantly being told how wonderful they are, then they will be perceived as successful whatever happens;
- a risk of cloning – if all high-flyers are matched against a high potential profile there is a chance that they will all exhibit the same characteristics (one company told us, for example, that they recruited 'pushy squirts' for their scheme);
- becoming elitist – if the scheme is viewed as a selective fast-track for the chosen few, then those who are not selected or who are

recruited too late can feel excluded and resentful, even if they have something positive to offer.

On the whole, if graduate development programmes and accelerated training for people with high potential are designed within the broader framework of a strategy on managerial succession, then they can often avoid such pitfalls. Moreover, if they are based on a robust view of potential and how it can be harnessed, they are more likely to meet their objectives.

Too often, however, organizations have a fast-track because it sounds dynamic and the sort of thing a 'thrusting' and successful company does. It is also felt to be good for motivation. In such cases it is rare for these organizations to conduct research to establish sound and reliable performance and potential criteria, let alone behavioural outcome statements.

Conclusion

We can see, therefore, that good practice in the area of managerial competence exists in some of the largest surveyed companies. We can also see that the techniques and approaches needed to extend this expertise more widely have existed for some time. If we are to be able to take this good practice forward into the next decade, then it is necessary for more organizations to be encouraged to embrace its principles of robustness more readily, and to reject the guesswork that has characterized practice during the 1970s and 1980s.

Reference

Hirsh, W. and Bevan, S. (1988), *What makes a manager?* (Brighton: Institute of Manpower Studies).

CHAPTER 2

Doubts about competency

JOHN BURGOYNE

Competency approaches have a valuable part to play in management development, but there are eight underlying problems or issues that any specific competency-based scheme must face up to. These are:

- whether performance can be divided into competences and then reintegrated,
- whether competences can be measured and whether appropriate methods exist,
- whether competency lists have universal relevance,
- how the ethical and moral content of professional management can be represented in competency lists,
- whether competency lists have a permanent value, given the changing nature of management,
- how different styles and strategies of managing can be accommodated,
- how managerial competences relate to the whole person,
- how individual competences contribute to and integrate into collective or organizational competence.

Overall, these eight issues suggest that a *mechanistic* application of a fragmented list of competences – all of which are based on generalized views of people, situations, organizations, industries and time – is inappropriate. Before examining each of these issues, however, it is important to explore the meaning of competency.

20

The concept of managerial competence

Competence can be defined simply as a manager's ability and willingness to perform a task. Such a definition is broadly compatible with most usages of the term. However, one special feature of management which will be explored later in the chapter arises from the notion of 'task'. Unlike non-managerial work, the nature of managing is to create and define its own task, rather than to tackle one that is prestructured. One of the attractions of competence is that it concerns doing and action, rather than the mere possession of knowledge. It is, however, a broader concept than skill and can usefully be thought of as encompassing knowledge, skill, understanding and will.

Another important distinction is that everyday usage of the term 'competence' often carries the connotation of 'mere competency', a minimal, scraping-through level of ability. This is not a helpful meaning to attach to the notion of managerial competence. Instead, the term is used within the business sector to express 'total quality'. A task is either done or it is not – there are no half measures.

There is very little difficulty in defining and defending a straightforward concept of total managerial competence. However, it does not automatically follow from this that it is appropriate to break down competence into lists of managerial competences that *may* be relatively universal and easily measurable. Nor does it necessarily follow that such lists are a useful foundation for a complete prescription for the delivery of management development.

Before this happens, the eight underlying issues mentioned above need careful consideration. Only then is it possible to move from a straightforward concept of managerial competence to one that incorporates management assessment and development methods. Each of the eight issues will now be examined.

Can performance be split into competences?

Research and commonsense show clearly that managing is not the sequential exercise of discrete competences. Managers do not use tools one at a time from the tool bag of managerial competences. Listings of separate competences at best simply

21

illuminate different facets of what is, at the end of the day, a complex whole.

It follows from this that using divided up lists of competences to manage with, to select managers by, or to develop managers against, creates the problem of how the separate list of competences is reintegrated into a holistic managerial performance. Learning separate aspects of managerial competence one at a time does *not* guarantee integral managerial performance. Neither can a manager who appears to possess separate managerial competences be guaranteed to be able to use them effectively.

Can competence be measured objectively?

Despite a vast amount of effort to discover this particular philosopher's stone, no straightforward, universal or acceptable technical method has emerged. Although extravagant claims are occasionally made about specific assessment systems, the fact is that if such a process is so easily used it would have caught on long ago.

There are theoretical grounds for believing that it is impossible to measure competency, just as there are theoretical grounds for knowing that it is not possible to turn base metal into gold by a chemical process. The fact that management or managing has to create and define its own task in which to be competent means that there cannot be prior objective criteria for its performance.

Managerial competences are best assessed by a process of informed and grounded judgement (as opposed to 'objective measurement'), by those who own and who are affected by the managerial action in question. This approach simply acknowledges the current reality of managerial practice and its assessment and suggests a realistic way for making it the basis for a rigorous process.

Universality

Much time and effort has been wasted on debating whether any two managerial jobs or situations are the same or different. The simple reality is that *all* managerial jobs are different at a detailed level of resolution. Similarly, *all* managerial jobs are the same at a high level of abstraction. Competency is of course exercised in discrete and specific situations, which means that each competent action will have its own mixture of idiosyncratic and shared elements. The paradox is that the more universally true any given list of competences is, the less immediately useful it is to any particular choice about how to act and behave in a specific situation.

The material question is what, if anything, of a universal nature is worth looking for or developing in managers. There are two very different kinds of competence that fit into this category which support situation-specific competences that apply in any given context. The underpinning competences are of a 'basic literacy', both of a literal and metaphorical type. They certainly include literacy, numeracy and basic analytical decision-making skills. There are certain concepts, techniques and approaches that, although man-made and changing in the long term, represent some basics which it is necessary to know to operate in a managerial community. Aspects of financial awareness and information technology are current examples. However, the basic literacy requirements of management change over time so any such listing needs continual revision.

The second kind, overarching competences, are those to do with being competent at learning, changing, adapting, forecasting, anticipating and creating change. These are the 'meta competences', which enable managers to create and adapt specific competences that underpin effective action in specific situations.

Moral, ethical, political and ideological aspects of management

The management world is clearly searching at the moment for an appropriate degree and form of professionalism. One of the general features of a professional code of conduct is its concern for its moral and ethical responsibilities to society, as well as for its technical efficiency and effectiveness.

Dealing with this issue simply through lists of managerial competency tends to emphasize the technical and to leave out the moral and ethical. If competency approaches are to become a major foundation for management development, ways must be found to expand and to accommodate the moral and ethical dimensions.

Value and mission statements are very much a part of *new age* organizations. These companies also tend to rely on individual identification with these values rather than bureaucratic procedures as ways of achieving coordination and integration of effort. Competent managing must involve engaging and mutually adjusting individual and organizational values.

The nature of managing

It is a matter of commonsense and observation that managerial competences differ, change and evolve from one era to another. The theoretical reason is that managerial work is always at the boundary between order and chaos, between what has not been done and what has already been done. Managing is literally a creative activity and like any creative activity its successful execution moves forward its boundary or frontier.

It follows from this that effective managerial performance exhausts or renders obsolete the competences that achieve this and brings new ones into play.

Many right ways to manage

Research and commonsense show that even in very specific situations there is more than one right way to manage. Any competence approach to management selection and development must be flexible and adaptive enough to be compatible with this reality.

Competent people

Being competent is different from having competences. Simply having competences begs the question of how they are used, who is the person using them and how he or she develops. If managerial competences are simply treated as a toolkit list, then this raises the question of who is the craft person, who is using the tools and what abilities they apply to their use.

The necessity of developing the whole person who operates within the managerial role cannot be driven out of any effective approach to management and management development.

Collective competence

Teams work effectively on the basis of complementary combinations of competence, exercised in a spirit of goodwill and cooperation in groups and organizations. High levels of individual member competence do not guarantee group or organizational competence and effectiveness. Indeed, if high levels of competence are associated with large egos, this may be a barrier to effective collaboration.

The implication of this point is that, even if businesses find effective ways of developing individual managerial competence, they still face the challenge of how to develop collective competence.

Conclusions and proposals

Reviewing competency approaches in the light of these eight underlying issues point towards the inappropriateness of the universal, mechanistic list of managerial competences. As an alternative, I suggest that any effective scheme must recognize:

- the holistic nature of management,
- the inevitability of a large element of judgement in its assessment,
- the variability of management across situations,
- the need to incorporate the moral, ethical element,
- the need to acknowledge that effective managing changes the nature of managerial competences,
- that there is more than one way to manage,
- that management development must attend to the whole person in the managerial role,

- that collective competency must be attended to in addition to individual competency.

All but the last point can be addressed by using the creative professions, rather than the technical professions, as the basic model for achieving a relevant degree of professionalism of management. This suggestion can be focused directly around the concept of the 'managerial portfolio'.

It is the custom in the creative professions to present portfolios of work as the basis for judging an individual's competence and abilities, as well as their own style, values and missions. In practice, managers and the managerial world naturally adopt this process. Managers considering the appointment of other managers tend to be more interested in accounts of their achievements than in profile information about their personalities. Encouraging managers to present themselves through the medium of their portfolios, possibly with some self-interpretation of the competences that the portfolio represents, and the kinds of situations and challenges that a specific portfolio qualifies a person for, may be the appropriate way forward for management and management development.

Such an approach to 'Certification of Management' would emphasize the qualitative nature of a manager's abilities, rather than some spurious claim to the achievement of some absolute and universal standards. A portfolio approach would keep entry into the managerial profession open and flexible, but rigorous. The managerial portfolio could provide a useful basis for developing agreements and discussion between individual managers and their employer organization about the combinations of formal training and work experience appropriate to fostering the depths and breadths of their competence and abilities. Such an approach would be a natural evolution and systematization of current natural management practice, rather than the imposition of an alien mechanistic process, which would, in all likelihood, be complied with or ignored.

CHAPTER 3

No simple answers

ROBIN JACOBS

Understanding and improving managerial performance has long been a difficult and sometimes controversial issue. Academics and practitioners alike have invested a considerable amount of time, effort and money in attempting to identify a logical and universally acceptable set of principles or structure that can be used to understand the determinants of successful managerial performance.

However, agreement has not been achieved on many of the central issues that appear to influence performance. As one might expect, this has been due in part to the difficulty involved in arriving at generally acceptable definitions in such a complex area. Nevertheless, it is also clear that the disagreement may also be due to the fact that, at a deeper level, the participants in the debate hold very different basic assumptions about the subject. They therefore arrive at quite different conclusions about how to define and develop managerial performance.

This chapter will concentrate on two different sets of assumptions about managerial performance, which represent opposite ends of a spectrum of beliefs about competence. The results of a recent survey conducted by the Ashridge Management Research Group on management assessment arrangements in the UK (1988) will also be discussed. The results appear to shed light on why these differences continue to exist. They also suggest that actively promoting a diversity of opinion and methods in this area may be beneficial to management development as a whole. Finally, some recommendations will be offered that it is hoped will help to indicate alternative directions and possibilities for the future of management development.

Traditional approaches to studying managerial performance

Research into managerial performance has a relatively long history, going back to the turn of the century. Much of it might be characterized, albeit rather crudely, by suggesting that it has attempted to understand performance by systematically reducing and simplifying complex human behaviour. For example, Frederick Taylor's ideas about scientific management and Henri Fayol's principles of management are landmark studies. They represent the belief that performance can best be understood by first fragmenting it and then analysing its basic constituent parts in order finally to develop a single set of universally appliccable principles. With one or two notable exceptions, much of what has followed over the years has embraced this basic philosophy. In other words, by applying so-called positivist research principles – simplification, quantification, logical analysis, deduction and so on – it is believed possible to arrive at a profound understanding of complex human behaviour.

The influence of this type of thinking has certainly had, and continues to have, widespread and popular appeal. For example, if asked what they know about research into the subject of motivation and leadership, I suspect that at the top of many managers' lists would be ideas like the motivation–hygiene theory, theory x and theory y, the 9:9 manager and so on. While such theories continue to have some currency, I also suspect that the same managers would agree that such ideas have given them little practical assistance in the complex business of improving managerial performance.

Despite the dominance and popular appeal of these over-simplifications of reality, there are signs of a growing unease about the authenticity and usefulness of this type of thinking. Business today is becoming increasingly turbulent and complex. The gap between reality and the functional ideas of much of the research into performance is visibly widening. Two recent publications by American management 'gurus' appear to recognize that fact and attempt to bridge the gulf. Both Tom Peters' *Thriving on Chaos* (1987) and Robert Quinn's *Beyond Rational Management* (1988) suggest that it is dangerous to deny that managerial life is highly complex and fraught with difficulties and ambiguities. They propose that we learn to live with the complexity and accept that we can never formulate complete, or once and for all, answers to the problems and issues involved. We must also apparently recognize that our understanding of performance will always be a partial view. Therefore, our concepts and definitions concerning performance must become more flexible and capable of accounting for the dynamic nature of management.

An alternative view of performance

While it is true that much of the research into managerial per- formance has promoted the idea that complex human behaviour can best be understood by applying functional logic, another view of the world is available. Indeed, like almost every other field of study, management contains two apparently opposing views, which have generated two very different perspectives about reality and truth. The realization, particularly in the physical sciences, that resolving complex problems often requires more than the application of rational principles is a clear example of the existence of this alternative thinking. Some of the most important scientific discoveries in the twentieth century owe far more to intuition, conceptualizing by analogy, imagination and the use of metaphor to describe the invisible than they do to the application of functional logic.

The social sciences are gradually beginning to recognize what disciplines such as quantum physics have known for many years – that the world cannot be known directly through the senses alone. It must increasingly include the invisible pattern of relationships within and between observable events. This is particularly true of the most complex phenomenon probably known to the human race – human behaviour. People cannot be studied effectively as if they were either animals or machines. We exist in a complex social environment. Our behaviour can only be interpreted meaningfully by accepting that an individual's behaviour depends in part on the way he or she understands a situation. It also depends on a vast range of personal qualities and attributes. From this perspective, specific social behaviour is directly related to idiosyncratic human features like aims, beliefs, reasons, plans, as well as perceived meanings. At this apparently deeper level of understanding, one is also forced to take seriously the widely differing life experiences of individuals and the fact that, to some extent, people are able to choose how they will achieve their goals.

In supporting this view, there is a need to accept that people perform successfully for different reasons at different times and under different sets of circumstances. Understanding managerial performance requires accepting that human behaviour is complex and dynamic.

The management competency approach

With its allusions to mere sufficiency and adequacy, the term competency itself seems to be of limited usefulness in a business world demanding excellence and outstanding performance. However, leaving that particular qualm aside for the moment, the development of the idea in the 1950s apparently came about as a reaction to earlier management research. This research was felt to be inadequate because it was unable to predict or suggest how managers' performances could be improved. Perhaps equally significant, such research had not benefited from the sophisticated data collection and analysis packages that characterize much of the recent research in the social sciences and management competency research in particular.

Briefly, the management competency approach attempts to describe performance by establishing a series of criterion-related factors, or constructs, of performance. The approach analyses attitudes about performance and statistically isolates apparently significant factors. By this method, its proponents believe that it is possible to identify objectively the most important dimensions of performance that successful managers need to be competent in. Some also believe that it is possible to establish dimensions of universal competence that are relevant across an entire organization and in other organizations as well. To some it would seem that what is being proposed is that the managerial abilities and skills identified through this method can almost be written on 'tablets of stone' within an organization. By implication at least, they can also be used as a reference point for that organization's entire human resource management programme, requiring perhaps only occasional and minor modification.

Doubts about competences

Two of the foremost American writers in the field (Byham and Thornton, 1982) state the objectives of the competency approach in a recent book. They suggest that its purpose is 'to identify clusters of behaviour that are specific, observable and verifiable, and that can be reliably and logically classified together'.

Is life or, more critically here, managerial behaviour really like that? The answer must be a resounding 'no'. While one cannot help but applaud any attempt to objectify behaviour, serious questions about the underlying assumptions of the approach should be raised. Useful data about performance can be gathered in this way but it must remain a very partial view of the world. The competency approach clearly has its roots firmly in the positivist traditions of research discussed earlier. This might be summarized crudely by the expression 'what you see is what you get'. In other words, if you can observe some piece of behaviour, you can then measure it and include it in any emerging model. But if you can't observe it, then it is probably not worth considering, let alone attempting to evaluate. This apparently overarching need to adhere strictly to 'scientific principles' has led to some conclusions that appear to be faintly bizarre.

For example, assessment centres are one of the most important practical outcomes of the approach. Here, managers' performances of simulated exercises are observed and evaluated according to a previously defined set of competences. Research has attempted to predict the future career progress of assessment centre candidates, based on their overall rating while attending the centre. So-called independent criterion measures have been sought to assess the validity of predictions about centre candidates and about the validity of the centre itself. One would have thought that some index of actual performance would have been most appropriate. Instead, measures of career progress like salary progression or promotion have been used. Unfortunately, in some organizations actual performance and career progress may, in fact, be largely unrelated.

31

Why then has career progress so often been chosen to measure the effectiveness and validity of assessment centres? The answer to this question seems reasonably plain to see. As discussed at length already, managerial performance is a complex phenomenon which is difficult to measure. By contrast, salary increases and promotions are relatively straightforward and reasonably easy to utilize. However, their connection to actual performance is an unreliable one. In a sense, their continued use as criterion measures, despite dubious evidence about their validity, gives insight into the whole underlying philosophy of the competency approach. Over-simplification and the complacent acceptance of other theoretical and methodological shortcomings appear to be tolerated so long as the need for practical measures is great enough. There can be little doubt about the vital nature of this particular need or about the fact that it will become increasingly more important as margins become tighter and the competition gets tougher. Surely then, there is even more reason for companies to examine the 'product' much more carefully than they appear to do before making the 'purchase'.

Another 'scientific' problem with assessment centres is that learning is likely to be taking place throughout the duration of the event. Indeed, certain individuals, while not performing well 'on the day', may have learnt a great deal from it. As a consequence, they actually begin to perform better back on the job. However, they may be denied certain career opportunities because of their apparent poor performance at the assessment centre. It is true that there is an increasing awareness of this particular problem among UK-based management development specialists. The use of 'development' centres is a clear example of the change of emphasis being given to competency-based assessment today. Nevertheless, there is a real and constant danger with the method of basing too many important decisions about people on what may be suspect data.

Another example of the problematical nature of the technique concerns a key area in assessment centres, the rating process. Paul Sacket (1982) came to some disturbing conclusions about this following some extensive research into the subject. He suggests that 'in looking at the rating process, one finds few dimensions contributing to the final evaluations, disagreement amongst assessors as to the importance of the various dimensions, extreme ratings being given weight in reaching consensus . . . etc'. In general, he recommends strongly that much more research is required into the technique if its results are to be taken seriously. In particular, he suggests that research is required into the dynamics of the assessor group and the way individuals form impressions and make decisions.

Considering the pressures on managers today to be successful in increasingly difficult and competitive world markets, their current enthusiasm for a technique that purports to guarantee an improvement in the quality of human resource decisions is understandable. Nevertheless, serious doubts about its validity and effectiveness, resulting from rigorously conducted research into the subject, are widespread. Its much vaunted scientific 'pedigree' appears to be more than a little suspect for those who care to investigate the 'product' in some detail. One final example of the problems involved is provided by Rice (1978), who has conducted detailed research in this area. He concludes that in general the management competency concept has not been well researched and is plagued by theoretical and methodological problems.

In a sense, its rapid acceptance in the UK (discussed later) might be seen as a good example of the effective 'niche' marketing of a product that is in need of considerable further development. For example, it is probably impossible to measure objectively important so-called 'soft' personal qualities like assertiveness, impact, creativity and sensitivity. They are therefore often omitted from competency-based assessment models. Does that mean that they should be considered as being less important or relevant than other measurable skills or qualities? Similarly, at senior levels of management, the political dimension of the job is generally reckoned to make significant demands on individuals. Would anyone seriously propose that this important area of skill can or should be measured objectively? The question is, of course, a rhetorical one. The point is that users of the competency approach should be aware that it provides a single and relatively partial view of the subject matter. Its emphasis on 'scientific' principles has led to a rather narrow and stilted perception of performance which appears incapable of fully reflecting the rich and often paradoxical nature of human behaviour.

33

Results of the Ashridge survey

One of the purposes of this chapter has been to show that the management competency method of assessing performance should be treated with some caution and care. However, it is not intended to suggest by this that the approach is unable to offer valuable practical insights into managerial performance. A recent survey of 500 organizations on the subject, conducted by the Ashridge Management Research Group (1988), provides evidence that there has been a surge of interest in the development of the technique involving many of the UK's largest companies. Nearly 70 per cent of the 100 large organizations contacted in the survey had some experience with it and a significant proportion of those had developed some sort of competency-based assessment only within the previous three years. Despite the shortcomings discussed earlier, the technique is clearly thought to be able to offer a better and more objective understanding of managerial performance than has been available in the past.

However, another interesting finding of the survey was that a small number of companies that had experience with the technique had decided that it was not entirely appropriate for their needs in this area. Furthermore, the companies concerned seemed to have much in common with one another. For example, they all appeared to be operating close to the so-called hi-tech revolution and perceived their markets and environment as turbulent and rapidly changing. Their relatively recent response to this realization has been to reorganize themselves into what might be described as loosely coupled, highly devolved businesses. Partly as a result of the environmental pressures and the devolved organization structures, their perception of the development needs of their managers has also changed. They now believe that they need to take more account of the different values and social processes that exist in different parts of the organization. In consequence, this has made it virtually impossible to define managerial performance and address development needs in a single and uniform way.

This recognition of the increasingly dynamic nature of managerial life in their organizations has led these companies to search for alternative ways to assess and develop the performance of their managers. The inappropriateness of developing long-lasting and uniform systems for managerial assessment and development in rapidly changing and evolving business environments appears to have been accepted by them. In one particularly intriguing reference to the experiences of management development specialists, life was seen to be like 'living out of tents'. The fast evolving and changing sets of demands being made for management development provision under these circumstances must indeed be difficult to manage. Nevertheless, extending the 'bedouin' analogy further, it is not being suggested that assessment and development for these companies should be seen as an attempt to 'clutch sand'. Instead, they appear to have recognized the need to develop alternative, more dynamic and flexible approaches to the problems and issues involved.

As part of this process, such companies are going to require assistance, perhaps initially at least, in the form of research that can identify more innovative techniques of assessment and development. For example, several of the companies involved suggested that the so-called 'soft' qualities of managers like creativity and sensitivity are going to be increasingly critical to their continued survival. Identifying approaches that are able to develop and assess such qualities is certainly going to be immensely challenging.

However, in the Ashridge survey, the majority of organizations believe their needs are being addressed quite effectively by the competency approach. In my opinion, these companies tend to be large, structured institutions which perceive that they are operating in relatively stable business environments. Consequently, they believe that management performance can, and should, be defined and measured in a single, uniform way. In a sense, because they perceive the nature of their business as being very predictable, they find the apparently systematic and rigorous methods involved in, for example, assessment centres quite attractive. It may also be that, partly because of the nature of their work and the slower pace of change being managed within such companies, the difficult 'soft' qualities of management are viewed as being relatively less important.

Taken overall, what the Ashridge research suggests is that different types of companies perceive the assessment and development needs of their managers differently. In fact, it is possible to suggest that a spectrum of opinion about the matter exists (see Figure 3.1).

35

At one end are the more traditional and long-established businesses like the banks and the oil companies. They seem to find particular value in adopting what might be termed the 'mainstream' functional approach to managerial assessment employed by the competency assessment movement. Moving towards the centre of the spectrum, we might place there some of the rapidly expanding high street retail chains. While several of them accept the basic competency idea and in some cases promote the widespread use of assessment centre technology, they are not all entirely convinced of its effectiveness. This has led some of them to experiment and adapt the technique to suit their specific needs. At the other end of the spectrum are the companies operating in the hi-tech related industries. These companies have begun to find that defining and setting solid benchmarks concerning individual managerial performance are much more difficult and have moved increasingly towards what might be termed the 'process' end. Here, 'living with ambiguity' and a concern for the impact of culture, personal values and qualities are almost a way of life.

While it is not being suggested that my interpretation of assessment arrangements is anything more than a map of general tendencies in the UK, it may be a useful method of broadly summarizing the way that in-company provision has developed. However, one important and additional insight should be included within this general picture. With the increasing internationalization

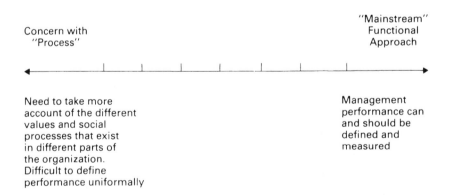

Figure 3.1 The wide spectrum of philosophies and approaches regarding competency assessment

of business and the advent of 1992 in Europe fast approaching, one might expect the balance of companies portrayed in the model to shift. Surprisingly, despite massive change being clearly visible on the immediate horizon, many managers do seem to view their position with some equanimity. However, it is likely that increasingly more companies will find their perceptions shifting from right to left across the spectrum as they begin to experience what the 'process'-oriented companies are now undergoing. I am referring to the perhaps uncomfortable realization that, in a turbulent business environment, successfully assessing and developing managerial performance involve a much more complex and difficult set of processes than proponents of the competency approach would have us believe.

To reiterate, designing long-lasting, relatively inflexible systems of assessment based on some narrowly formed assumptions about performance is likely to be increasingly inappropriate and perhaps eventually redundant. More and more companies may begin to find that they too are going to require more innovative, less rigidly defined and structured methods of managerial assessment and development.

Overall, what I am suggesting is that a contingency approach to assessment and development is essential for the continued success of businesses. In other words, companies must become more sensitive to the demands of their specific situation before investing heavily in a particular assessment methodology. In the short term, at least, this is likely to create a demand for the wide diversity of approaches identified earlier.

New directions

One of the most comprehensive and up-to-date surveys of managerial assessment (Byham and Thornton, 1982) suggests strongly that several different methods are indeed necessary for a complete assessment of managerial abilities and furthermore that 'each of the methods can provide unique insights into managerial potential or competence'.

I would obviously support that contention but would want to change the emphasis given from 'necessary' to 'essential' for complete assessment, etc. Given the widely differing sets of perceived and actual business circumstances that companies find themselves in, alternative assessment ideas should not simply be seen as merely supplementary to 'traditional' competency thinking. If useful alternatives are forthcoming and we accept the contingency argument, then in some cases they should take the place of what is fast becoming the traditional method of performance assessment.

There are, of course, problems involved in developing alternative assessment methods that attempt to account for the complexity and ambiguity in managerial performance in a serious manner. For instance, they are unlikely to be driven exclusively by the need to be purely objective and rational in their approach. Instead, they are likely to emphasize the subjective nature of organization life, take some account of the irrationality and unpredictability of personal feelings and in general attempt to represent a range of perceptions about a manager's performance.

The more profound and complex nature of the type of research required to develop such alternatives may not have the kind of immediate popular appeal and support that the more functional methods have generated. This fact should not in itself discourage managers from actively supporting and promoting it. By not focusing exclusively upon objectivity and rationality, the alternative approaches are also likely to be heavily criticized by some supporters of the competency approach.

With the growing interest in self-development by management development specialists, one fruitful avenue for research might lie in self-assessment models. In a recent article, Fletcher (1984) argues that research has shown the viability of self-assessment. He believes that distortion and bias creep into judgements about performance no matter who does the judging. He recommends a form of structured self-appraisal focusing on different parts of an individual's job. Furthermore, he notes that the Gulf Oil company has developed this approach. It now includes the perceptions of superiors, subordinates, peers and the appraisees themselves in the final assessment of an individual's performance. He concludes his article by suggesting that 'our perceptions of what is real and valid in the world rest on a consensus of shared beliefs. Appraisals of performance are not an exception to that rule.'

Support for the self-assessment and shared perceptions idea was also evident in more recent research by this author (Jacobs and Everett, 1988). In a study of perceptions about performance in senior manager teams, several important conclusions were reached about the processes and likely pay-offs involved in sharing peer perceptions at this level. Overall, the research's most important recommendation was a relatively simple one. In the absence of valid, independent criterion measures of output at this level, a structured sharing of perceptions of individual performance within the peer group setting may provide a relatively authentic and viable measure of senior manager performance. The concept has been developed into a consultancy tool to be used with groups of senior managers.

There seems to be a willingness amongst some companies to experiment with new and more innovative ideas in this area. If, as many organizations have suggested, effective methods of managerial assessment and development provide them with a major competitive advantage, then research and development in this area must be supported. Furthermore, any new research is likely to be characterized by a shift away from a strictly rational and functional view of managerial performance. Instead, it should give emphasis to a more particularist view which is, in turn, likely to take more account of the subjective values, beliefs and perceptions of an organization's managers. In doing so, it is far more likely to provide a dynamic and forward-looking perspective on performance than the rather static and retrospective view generated by the management competency approach.

Conclusion

I have attempted to show that assessing and developing managerial performance is a complex and difficult endeavour for which there is unlikely to be a single or simple set of answers. With the considerable investment being made on behalf of the Management Charter Group initiative in Britain in particular, there is a need to examine the basic assumptions and beliefs of the participants in the continuing debate about how to proceed. It would seem that the favoured approach – the management competency model – employs a relatively narrow and traditionally 'scientific' philosophy. While such a systematic approach is always likely to have popular appeal, it contains definite weaknesses. Also, in common with every 'map' of reality, it must remain a very partial representation of the truth. Therefore, claims concerning its universal appropriateness and relevance should be viewed with scepticism.

References

Ashridge Management Research Group (1988), Council for National Academic Awards/Training Agency Survey of Current Practice in Assessing Management Competences, September.

Byham, W. C. and Thornton, G. C. (1982), *Assessment Centres and Managerial Performance* (New York: Academic Press).

Fletcher, C. (1984), What's new in performance appraisal, *Personnel Management*, February, pp 20-2.

Jacobs, R. C. and Everett, J. G. (1988), 'The importance of team building in a hi-tech environment', *Journal of European Industrial Training*, May.

Peters, Tom (1987), *Thriving on Chaos* (New York: Alfred A. Knopf).

Quinn, R. E. (1988), *Beyond Rational Management – Mastering the Paradoxes and Competing Demands of High Performance* (San Francisco: Jossey Bass).

Rice, B. (1978), 'Measuring executive muscle', *Psychology Today*, December, pp 95–110.

Sacket, P. R. (1982), 'A critical look at some common beliefs about assessment centres', *Public Personnel Management Journal*, November, pp. 140–7.

CHAPTER 4

Unravelling managerial performance

TOM BOYDELL

The notion of 'competency' is complex since it covers a number of sets of attributes that appear similar but are actually different. The picture is further complicated by the fact that, although these sets are indeed different and independent, they are at the same time related.

My consultancy, TRANSFORM, has been exploring for some time the nature of these attributes and the way in which they are connected. We have used four sources for this study, namely:

* extensive data from research with a number of managers across a wide range of organizations;
* established models from mainstream developmental psychology;
* models specifically related to management development developed by colleagues in NPI, based in Holland, and in TRIGON, based in Austria;
* underpinning archetypes from the work of Rudolf Steiner and anthroposophical psychology, with further development of these by Bernard Lievegoed (1973).

Strands or clusters of competence

We can often gain insights into the nature of something by an examination of the etymology or derivation of the word itself.

41

The photofit manager

Competence comes from the Latin, *competere*, to come together. This word in turn is made of *com*, together, and *petere*, to seek. So the nature of competence is to do with things coming together. Indeed, in our own modern language we have the phrase 'so-and-so has got it all together', to describe someone who is performing particularly well.

So competence is about bringing things together, not about splitting them up into minute portions. However, it is still useful to examine the separate components before seeing what they look like when combined.

At the moment our own research suggests three quite distinct (yet related) clusters or strands of competence, namely:

- seven managerial activities,
- seven modes of managing,
- seven personal qualities.

To start with, we will look at each cluster in turn, and then examine their relation to each other.

Managerial activities

In this first of the three clusters or strands of competence we have the following seven fundamental activities of managing. These are:

* handling physical resources to get things done
* controlling the processes and systems that get things done
* creating conditions that enable and empower people to get things done
* meeting together in such a way that the people who are going to get things done really meet each other properly
* picturing the future of what the people want for the organization; making a choice between possible alternatives
* forming policies that guide the way things are done
* focusing the purpose of the organization – what it is here for, why it wants to do things.

We believe that this is a general model of managerial activity. It differs from models of 'functional activity' because it is intended

42

to be valid across all functions (such as production and marketing, etc.).

These managerial activities are mutually distinct and may be learned independently of each other through appropriate processes of management and organization development.

Modes or ways of managing

These ways of managing are described in detail in Leary *et al.* (1986). The basic nature of these is expressed in the term 'mode', which means a 'way or manner of acting, doing, happening, or existing; . . . a state of being' (*Chambers Twentieth Century Dictionary*). Thus, the mode of managing that I am in at a particular time is my state of being or existence. This state thoroughly permeates everything I do as a manager.

Unlike the managerial activities, these modes are not entirely independent of each other. Rather, they form a progression and develop in sequence one after the other. Just as a plant develops in sequence of root, shoot, leaf and then flower, so mode 1 is followed by mode 2, then mode 3 and so on (see Figure 4.1).

The seven modes of managing are:

* *adhering* to rules, procedures and 'givens' in a situation
* *adapting* to rules, procedures and 'givens'
* *relating* to norms, conventions and ideas

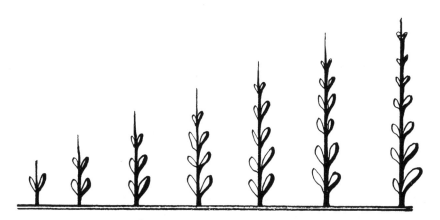

Figure 4.1

The photofit manager

* *experiencing* yourself
* *experimenting* to deepen, improve and test out
* *integrating* to form large-scale, holistic connections and over-
  views
* *dedicating* yourself to an external purpose.

As already stated, each mode has to be developed as a distinct way of being in a particular sequence. However, the process is not so much like climbing a ladder but more like the growth of a plant. In this way, competence in mode 1 must appear before mode 2. However, further growth *within* mode 1 can occur while mode 2 is developing. Similarly, while mode 3 is appearing, further growth can be taking place in modes 2 and 1.

Again, like a plant, the earlier modes of competence are still available for use when appropriate. They are not discarded as they all have a useful role to play.

Personal qualities

Finally, the third dimension or strand of competence is a cluster of inner, personal qualities which the individual can bring to managerial work. In our model these may be listed as:

* stability
* control
* sensitivity and awareness
* sense of self and independence
* seeking, striving and deepening
* connecting and widening
* sense of purpose.

These personal qualities are brought out through appropriate processes of self-development. Unlike the other modes of competence, this does not take place in a particular sequence or progression. Therefore an alternative depiction may be useful, as in Figure 4.2, particularly as this shows how the seven qualities may be complementary pairs (not polar opposites), with a balancing, harmonizing quality in the centre.

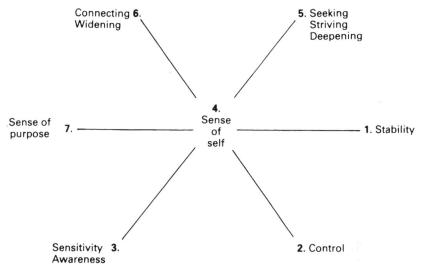

Figure 4.2

How the three strands form managerial competence

We have used the word 'strand' quite deliberately to suggest an analogy with a rope. The latter is a whole in itself – it is the whole rope that carries out its function, and it is perceived as a whole. At the same time, it is made up of a number of strands that can, if we so wish, be unravelled and looked at separately. In terms of bringing the strands together, they interrelate as follows.

First, particular managerial activities need to be carried out in specific modes. For example:

- handling physical resources requires the adhering mode
- controlling processes and systems requires the adapting mode
- creating conditions requires the relating mode
- meeting together requires the experiencing mode
- picturing the future requires the experimenting mode
- forming policies requires the integrating mode
- focusing the purpose requires the dedicating mode.

At the same time, each mode calls on a particular personal quality (see Figure 4. 3). For example:

45

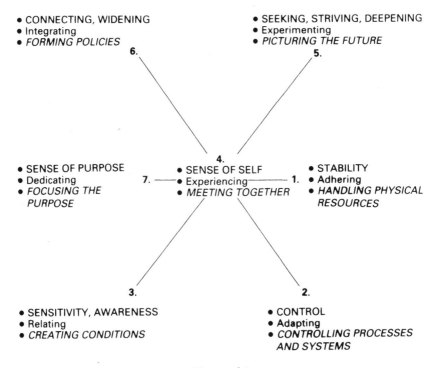

Figure 4.3

- adhering requires stability
- adapting requires control
- relating requires sensitivity and awareness
- experiencing requires a sense of self and independence
- experimenting requires seeking, striving and deepening
- integrating requires connecting and widening
- dedicating requires a sense of purpose.

To be 'fully competent', you need a full repertoire of modes, based on a full set of personal qualities, applied to a full range of managerial activities (See Table 4.1).

The independent nature of each strand

We have shown that 'competence' is the bringing together of different strands. At the same time, each of these is separate,

Table 4.1 Repertoire of competence modes

MANAGERIAL ACTIVITY is done in the	MODE of and requires the	PERSONAL QUALITY of
1 Handling physical resources	Adhering	Stability
2 Controlling processes and systems	Adapting	Control
3 Creating conditions	Relating	Sensitivity, awareness
4 Meeting together	Experiencing	Sense of self, independence
5 Picturing the future	Experimenting	Seeking, striving, deepening
6 Forming policies	Integrating	Connecting, widening
7 Focusing the purpose	Dedicating	Sense of purpose
Management and organization development	Manager development	Self-development

independent and on a distinct dimension of its own.

It will be noticed that each of the three clusters or strands has been depicted so far as containing seven elements, pivoting around the fourth. Expressed another way, there are three elements above the centre one, and three below it. These elements can be presented in a different form, starting with the seven managerial activities.

Managerial activities: the space dimension

Here we can turn the seven activities upside-down so that they read as follows:

7 focusing the purpose
6 forming policies
5 picturing the future
4 meeting together
3 creating conditions
2 controlling processes and systems
1 handling physical resources.

It will be seen that the top three are all things that primarily exist within people's heads: they are ideas; pictures; dreams; values and principles. Conversely, the bottom three are all concrete, physical and material. Put another way, the people who meet together in the middle engage in the non-material activities 'above the line', and then convert these into material reality 'below the line'.

This dimension is sometimes referred to as that of 'ideas–reality'. However, this misunderstands the nature of ideas, as in fact these *are* real as well. Therefore the true nature of this dimension is that of 'spiritual reality–material reality' or, more simply, of spiritual–material. Another way of expressing this is to say that it is the space dimension, since everything exists in space – material space or spiritual space.

This leads to the need to work with the seven managerial activities. It is, of course, vital to ensure that the material, physical aspects of the organization (i.e. the three 'below the line') match the ideas, values, etc. that come from the spiritual realities above the line. Put another way, the conditions, processes/systems and physical resources must be consistent and compatible with the picture of the future, as well as with the policies, purpose and desired identity of the organization.

Conversely, if we want to know about an organization's actual, current vision, policies and identity (which may or may not be what is written down in official documents, mission statements and the like), we can see these reflected in the prevailing conditions, processes/systems and physical resources.

In general, therefore, we find that:

* at any given time, the actual vision, policies and identity will be reflected in the current conditions, processes/systems and physical resources;
* when consciously working to change the vision, policy and identity we will have to make corresponding changes to conditions, processes/systems and physical resources;
* when making conscious changes to conditions, processes/systems and physical resources, we need to take into account the fact that these are a reflection of the organization's actual and/or stated vision, policies, and identity.

In this way, we need to be engaged in a constant flow, above the line, below the line, above the line, below the line, and from spiritual to material to spiritual to material, etc.

This is a transformation process. The spiritual is transformed into the material; the material is transformed into the spiritual. Each must be contained into the other, or rather, each is always contained in the other. What we must do is to bring this mutual containment into full consciousness at all times. This flowing process is depicted in Figure 4.4. It will be seen that we have also shown not only the general reflection of the top three in the bottom three, and vice versa, but also particular links between the processes/systems; purpose/identity and physical resources. We will return to these particular linkages later.

Modes of managing: the time dimension

People who are operating in each of the first three modes are in some way attaching themselves to parameters that are external

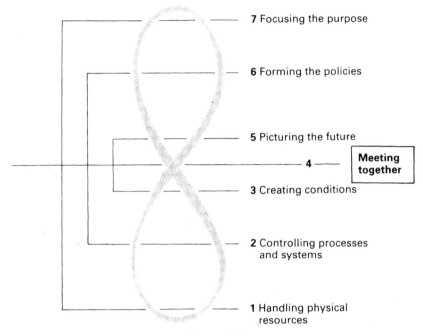

Figure 4.4

to themselves and that have been handed down in the past by somebody else. They are either adhering (mode 1) or adapting (mode 2) to previously set rules, guidelines, procedures, given ways of doing things, or relating to ideas and parameters that have previously been worked out, thought through and explained. In mode 4, when I am experiencing myself, I am in the present. Modes 5, 6 and 7 are to do with the future – with moving forward to deepen my knowledge (mode 5), making connections (mode 6), and achieving my purpose in life (mode 7).

This, therefore, is the time dimension, as depicted in the left-to-right version of the modes in Figure 4.5. This illustrates that, just as particular pairs of the seven managerial activities are particularly connected, so there are special links between certain modes.

For example, dedicating yourself to your external purpose requires tenacity and the willingness to stick with things when the going gets rough. These are similar characteristics to those associated with adhering, albeit in a different form.

50

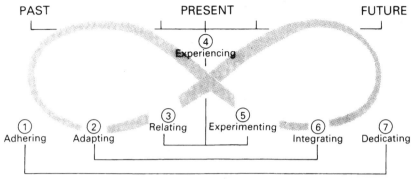

Figure 4.5

Again, there is a superficial similarity between integrating and adapting. Both involve a certain quality that in the latter is perhaps best described as canniness, cunning and 'street skills'. These stem from individuals who are able to notice how particular phenomena happen together and give rise to each other. However, this is purely empirical and in no way involves the questioning of *why* these things should be connected. They are also restricted to things that involve short-term personal benefit. In the integrating mode, these qualities are transformed into true wisdom, with a mixture of very deep understanding together with very wide, holistic connections. Managers in this mode tend to operate in a massively broader timescale and rarely consider how to manipulate circumstances to their own advantage. It is interesting to note that in our research nearly all the managers who described themselves as operating in mode 6 were, in our view, in reality in mode 2.

Finally, there is a certain similarity between relating and experimenting. Both require a degree of curiosity – a need to know why things are as they are. This is in contrast to modes 1 and 2 where, as already stated, there is no interest in the reasons that lie behind phenomena. The difference is that in mode 3, relating, this curiosity is satisfied by reference to other people's explanations derived from the past. But in experimenting, mode 5, people try to find their own answers by testing and trying out. In this way they take a step into the future.

We have here, then, another transformation process. For example:

● adhering can be transformed into dedicating and dedicating requires transformed aspects of adhering;

- adapting can be transformed into integrating and integrating requires transformed aspects of adapting;
- relating can be transformed into experimenting and experimenting requires transformed aspects of relating;
- the past can be transformed into the future and the future requires transformed aspects of the past.

Personal qualities: the soul dimension

As already described, these are *inner* qualities that lie in the individual's soul. (This is, of course, only one meaning of the term 'soul'. In anthroposophical psychology it is 'that which thinks, feels, desires, etc . . . the innermost being or nature', to quote the *Chambers'* dictionary. Other terms are used, namely 'ego or spirit'.)

However, these inner qualities are in themselves of no use. They need to be brought forth to bear on one's activities in the *outer* world. This is therefore the inner–outer dimension. For example:

- inner qualities are transformed when they are used in the outer world;
- outer behaviours are transformed when we bring inner qualities to bear on them.

We have already seen that these inner personal qualities may be shown as complementary pairs.

The final link

We have, therefore, the three independent dimensions of competence illustrated in Figure 4.6. These are:

SPACE: up–down – the seven managerial activities
TIME: back–front – the seven modes of managing
SOUL: inside–outside – the seven personal qualities

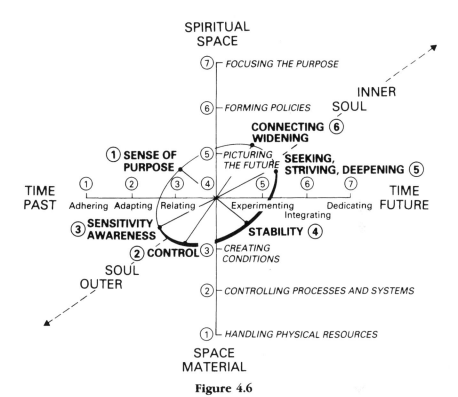

Figure 4.6

Management and organizational transformation involves turning
  things upside down and downside up.

Manager transformation involves working in such a way as to turn
  things back to front and front to back.

Self-transformation involves working in such a way as to turn things
  inside out and outside in.

The photofit manager

We have already seen how each dimension may be viewed as an integral strand of a whole 'rope' of competence. We can take this further, to show that although independent (Figure 4.7) they are none the less connected by certain fundamental attributes. These connections, which are due to fundamental archetypes that lie behind each of the three dimensions, are manifested in the way that each of them may be seen as comprising linked pairs (as has already been described). This can be illustrated in the alternative ways in Figures 4.6, 4.7 and 4.8.

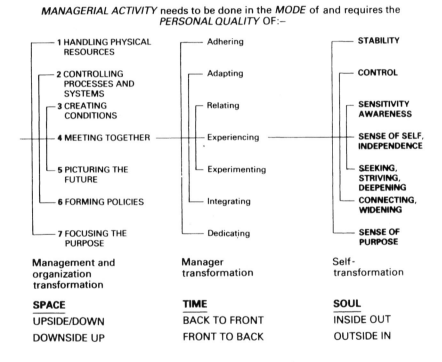

Figure 4.7

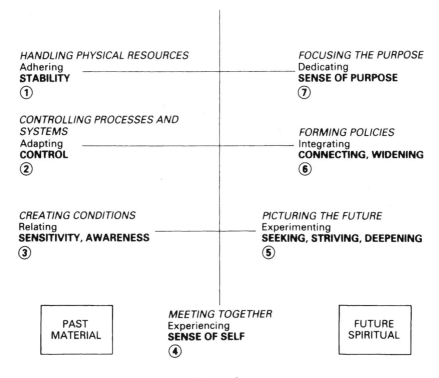

Figure 4.8

References

Leary, M., Boydell, T., van Boeschoten, M. and Carlisle, J. A. (1986), *The Qualities of Managing* (Sheffield: Manpower Services Commission).
Lievegoed, B. (1973), *The Developing Organization* (Millbrae, Calif.: Celestial Arts).

CHAPTER 5

Individual and collective competency

CHARLES DODD

Psychometric tests cannot give all the answers about managerial performance but they can provide useful insights and a depth of information to help individuals to make better decisions for themselves. At the same time, psychometric tests can save organizations from grim and costly mistakes.

Belbin's team roles

Thousands of tests and questionnaires are available (or not available, thanks to the sensibly exacting restrictions on access, particularly by the British Psychological Society and test publishers Toplis *et al.*). Choosing the right test has recently been compared to crossing a minefield to purchase a used car (Kerr Brown Associates, 1987, p. 4). Certainly the process of selection can be hazardous, even foolhardy, and the eventual prize may turn out not to be a runner. The Belbin team roles inventory is, however, a safe and straightforward choice for a range of business purposes.

Many people have used (and too many have abused) the earlier versions of the self-perception questionnaire (Belbin, 1981). Management colleges and practitioners frequently include the questionnaire in a course or a consultancy. It is also accessible to the generalist as well as the specialist. As Antony Jay reminds us, Dr Meredith Belbin's work is based on an original concept, rigorously developed and tested, to give results that are validated by successful prediction and applications that go to the very heart of management (Belbin, 1987, p. vii).

Many psychometric tests of personality are designed to measure traits. The questionnaires that Dr Belbin has developed offer ways of identifying and analysing how traits manifest themselves as behaviour, especially in groups and teams. The theory (and the evidence) is that the number of team-roles is finite. Initially seven, then eight roles were identified and now the total stands at nine. It seems unlikely to increase beyond this number, although there have been three changes of terminology: the chairman role has become coordinator (because it is sexist, and too many people want to be chairman?); implementer is the new name for company worker (after all, who would choose to be labelled as the company worker?); and the plant role has become innovator.

The full list is now innovator (IN), resource investigator (RI), monitor evaluator (ME), coordinator (CO), shaper (SH), implementer (IMP), team worker (TW), completer–finisher (CF) and specialist (SP). Details are given in the User's Manual (Belbin Associates, 1988, pp. 5–13; see also Belbin, 1987, especially pp. 65–78).

Cambridgeshire County Council recognized the potential of the new Belbin system (INTERPLACE) and has contributed to its development. As the first user of the system during its trial period, the County Council has had some influence on shaping the final version and now uses it extensively for a range of functions.

Self-perception

The *self-perception inventory* takes about 20 minutes to complete. Most people find it an intriguing and slightly challenging experience. The raw scores are entered on computer files through the INTERPLACE program and are converted through norms to a graphic display of a percentage chart. This shows an individual's natural team roles, the roles that are best avoided and any others which can make up the middle ground (Table 5.1).

The photofit manager

To quote from Belbin's User's Manual (Belbin Associates, 1988, p. 23): 'The mark at the bottom (DR) refers to points dropped in the *self-perception inventory* which would otherwise have been available to the nine team roles. In effect the DR scale is based on responses to a control item in each section of the SPI. Each item sounds attractive but has no real bearing in valued team roles. A high score is indicative of an unrealistic self-image and is taken into account in the output of the system. The DR score can be displayed and printed or not according to requirements.'

In addition to the graph, the data from the SPI also generates a narrative report. For example, the scores in Table 5.1 translate into a *character profile and placement guidance* (Table 5.2).

Observer assessment

The cautionary note at the head of a character profile draws attention to the fact that the narrative is based on limited evidence. As indicated, the views of at least four people who know the individual should be taken into account. Typically these people might be the person's colleagues, manager or subordinates.[1] Their viewpoints are sought through a new questionnaire consisting of lists of positive and negative statements, in the form of adjectives, which translate into team roles. Table 5.3 is an example of someone whose self-perception of his natural roles is coordinator, innovator and implementer. However, this profile has been adjusted by six observers to completer–finisher, coordinator and implementer.

In Table 5.3, the team roles have not been drastically adjusted by the observers and the consequent profile is *filled out* rather than radically altered. On occasions and for a variety of reasons, the differences between self-perception and the observers' assessment (OA) can be very considerable. Investigating these differences is often a profitable process. A small difference may be because the individual has a fairly clear self-image and communicates it openly to colleagues. However, a large difference may illuminate problems in a team – whether the difference arises from a misperception by the individual or by the observers. Exploration

Table 5.1 An example of a self-perception team role profile

	Roles best avoided			Roles able to be assumed				Natural roles			
	0	10	20	30	40	50	60	70	80	90	100
IN										X	
RI		X									
CO		X									
SH										X	
ME								X			
TW					X						
IMP			X								
CF					X						
SP				X							
DR		X									

Table 5.2 An example of a character profile and placement guidance

Please note that this report is based on fewer than four observers' assessments and should therefore be treated with caution.

This individual:

- has innovative tendencies and needs to work in a mentally challenging environment
- could be good at solving complex problems
- is likely to be drawn to work that exercises his mind
- is someone who thinks before acting
- has a discriminating mind
- needs to be in a job where he has some authority
- is likely to thrive on confrontation and debate
- needs to learn to manage people with patience.

Table 5.3   Comparing self-perception with observers' assessment

---

1   *Self-perception:*

- has innovative tendencies and needs to work in a mentally challenging environment
- above average in terms of self-organization and control
- has an interest in taking on a coordinating role.

2   *Adjusted by observers' assessment:*

- generally regarded as an individual who is challenging
- has an eye for detail
- patient when dealing with routine work
- very precise and achieves high standards
- above average in terms of self-organization and control
- should be able to tackle most jobs methodically
- has an interest in taking on a coordinating role
- should not be involved in work where motivating people is important.

Note: The adjectives most frequently ticked by the observers in this example were 'challenging', 'disciplined', 'aware of priorities', 'thorough', 'hard-driving', 'critical', 'fussy'. Altogether there were 88 adjectival responses from six observers.

of the gap could well contribute to the development of the team.

Job requirement

Another major addition to the earlier revisions of the questionnaire is the *job requirement exercise* (JRE). This exercise is a means of defining the competences of the 'round hole' into which the 'square peg' (as defined by the SPI and preferably the OA) fits or does not fit.

The various competences are grouped into 'task demands' – 'dealing with people'; those required by 'work conditions and con-straints'; and 'demands on mental ability, experience and training'. As the User's Manual carefully explains (Belbin Associates, 1988, p. 25): 'The compatibility between a certain job and a candidate is measured by *shape* . . . whether a certain candidate has the right job experience or the right special skills . . . must be assessed separately through interview, examination of track record and/or with the aid of the relevant tests of ability. What INTERPLACE will do, however, once a person's eligibility is ascertained, is to inform you if the candidate's character shape is well suited to that particular job.'

Table 5.4 gives an example of reports on two candidates applying for a post that called for the team roles of resource investigator, innovator and coordinator.

Table 5.4 Candidates' compatibility with the job

1   X is a poor fit with the job specification:

He is perhaps too inward looking and too slow moving for the demands of this particular job. He shows a creative disposition and has the right profile for initiating new developments and making original contributions. On the other hand, he may lack the necessary interest in organizing or controlling other people to be really effective in this job.

Overall, his profile is innovator, shaper and monitor evaluator.

2   Y is a very good fit with the job specification:

She seems to have the qualities needed for the exploratory part of the job and has the ability to negotiate and sell. She should be sufficiently outgoing to meet the job demands. She shows a creative disposition and has the right profile for initiating new developments and making original contributions. She should be able to cope well with coordinating people and steering group effort. She is likely to make an effective contribution to working out priorities and formulating worthwhile goals.

Overall, her profile is innovator, resource investigator and coordinator.

Recruitment and selection

Most people claim to be good at recruiting and selecting. However, all too often bad decisions are made and organizations are stuck with useless employees for years to come. Making the wrong decision at recruitment can be very expensive and very damaging, yet companies continue to rely almost totally on the interviewing process.

A recent review of selection methods[2] produced some startling results. In the examples studied, the predictive validity of interviews was only about 15 per cent (not much more than the validity of graphology or astrology). On the other hand, the use of personality and ability tests led to sound results two to three times more often.

No doubt best of all is the combination of testing with interviewing, which reinforces relatively objective measurement with subjective impressions.

As has already been indicated, the validity of a self-perception questionnaire is open to challenge (particularly when individuals are competing for an appointment). Belbin's SPI carries the appropriate words of caution and it makes sense to monitor the self-perception through several OAs, where this is feasible. But the very nature of external recruitment and selection limits the opportunities for informed observers to contribute to an assessment. The combination of SPI and OA is more feasible for internal promotion boards or when an organization uses an assessment centre. The latter in particular gives an opportunity for fairly protracted observation.

However, even when the OA cannot be used, the completion of the job requirement exercise is worthwhile. It is proving to be a searching and robust questionnaire.[3] The competences seem to be the appropriate ones for a wide range of middle and senior management posts and the process of completing the form (often best done by a few people separately and then in a group to share views and reconcile differences) is a powerful way of focusing on the essentials of a job. Working through the exercise also guards one from the danger of the test determining the job rather than the other way round. This is a real risk with the proliferation of tests and the comparative neglect of job definition. Indeed, job analysis has been accurately described as the most neglected part of the process of recruitment and selection (Incomes Data Services, 1985).

Team analysis and development

When individuals have been singled out for an appointment, it is not long before they are drawn into work groups and teams. Organizations seem unable to function without a vast mesh of these groups. Definitions of a team (when is a group a team?) usually include a common purpose, a will to work together and a mix of skills, experience and (perforce) personality. The mix may bring problems as well as advantages. It should be recognized that, especially at the strategic level in an organization, the interplay of personality can be the most effective or the most destructive constituent in a team. Judicious analysis will expose problems and may lead to their resolution.

Descriptions and diagnoses of successful and unsuccessful teams can be found in Belbin's standard work on the subject (Belbin, 1987, passim). I have found the combination of the SPI and the OA exercises very useful, both as an analytical tool and as a process for team development. I have yet to meet a team that is less than eager to learn about itself. Also, sharing information derived from the two questionnaires can in itself move a group closer together and encourage it to both address and solve problems.

Table 5.5 is an example of the SPI plus OA exercise which was administered to a team of seven middle managers in a large service organization. The exercise revealed a definite pattern of natural team roles. One possible analysis of the team profile might go like this: some ideas here certainly, but this may be an inward-looking group. Is there uneasiness about who should run the meetings? (Four coordinators in a group of seven people could be counterproductive.) The absence of teamworking and the emphasis on implementing and completing could be worth exploring – do they have a distorting effect, or are the tasks of the team ones that call mostly for the practical and the painstaking?

Table 5.5 Example of natural team roles among seven middle managers

Innovator	2
Resource investigator	–
Coordinator	4
Shaper	1
Monitor evaluator	3
Team worker	–
Implementer	4
Completer-finisher	5
Specialist	1

During discussion these observations were found to be relevant. They were also illuminated by a quick scan of the responses to the OA, which revealed (in terminology taken from the questionnaire) that the group's view of its own culture could be described as conscientious, accurate, efficient, aware of priorities, disciplined, painstaking, perceptive, thorough and professional. However, it was also impatient, critical, fussy, territorial and frightened of failure.

The benefits of Belbin in practice

Besides the expected improvements in the recruitment process and in team development, some unforeseen and intriguing benefits from the three questionnaires are emerging.

Meredith Belbin has drawn my attention to the value of using INTERPLACE to increase people's self-insight in those situations where they 'play out of role' or are in conflict with the roles of other team members. In particular, an individual can learn much from practising a secondary team-role – in effect, 'making a team-role sacrifice' by temporarily giving up his or her primary role in the interest of the whole group. This may also have the useful consequence of 'creating a team-role void' for a colleague to fill. Thus, a coordinator who is not very keen to take the role of completer–finisher may sacrifice his or her primary role of CO and deliberately work at developing CF skills, thereby allowing another who needs practice at coordinating to fill the ensuing space.

At a time of escalating interest in the identification and development of the skills of management and some random and even frantic theorizing, INTERPLACE has been found to work well in practice. The system sheds a clear, sharp light on several of the vexing features of managerial competence and organization development.

Notes

1 See the recent finding from research in the United States (as reported in *The Financial Times*, 9 November 1988, p. 20) that four out of every five subordinates' ratings and managers' self-valuations 'were much more in agreement with one another than the manager's boss was with either . . . it's easier to fool the guy you work for than the people who work for you'.

2 Based on work carried over by Ivan Robertson and Roger Makin of UMIST, as reported (for example) in Herriott (1987).

3 The author has given the Belbin practice example for the JRE (the job of a GP) to various individuals and groups. The results are uncannily consistent.

References

Belbin Associates (1988), *INTERPLACE: matching people to jobs.*
Belbin, R. Meredith (1981), *Management teams: why they succeed or fail* (London: Heinemann).
Belbin, R. Meredith (1987), *Management teams: why they succeed or fail.* (London: Heinemann, reprint).
Incomes Data Services Ltd (1985), *Study of psychological assessment*, Study 341, July, p. 8.
Kerr Brown Associates (1987), *Update*, Winter.
Toplis, John, Dulewicz, Vic and Fletcher, Clive (1987), *Psychological testing: a practical guide for employers* (London: Institute of Personnel Management).

Filling in the detail: developing leaders and teams

Introduction

In a practical case study in Chapter 6, Brian O'Neill describes how British Airways uses competences to assess and develop senior managers. In the process, the company has encountered many of the issues and dilemmas raised in Section 1. The company acknowledges, for example, the difficulty of ensuring that competency profiles keep pace with the changing nature of management. Recognizing that this weakness can never be fully overcome, BA none the less advocates *proactive profiling*, where competences are tightly entwined around past research, long-term business forecasts and corporate strategy.

In addition, O'Neill emphasizes the need for *competency compensation*, an approach that recognizes that not every manager measures up to idealized lists. The ultimate aim is to produce flexible, well rounded and diverse leaders – not clones.

Other issues raised in this chapter include how competences can become a shared language across the organization and inspire growth and change; how to overcome the problem of imposing an absolute standard of performance on specialists lacking management experience; and how to strike a balance between academic aptitude and practical experience.

ICI's approach to competency sharply contrasts with that of British Airways and echoes Burgoyne and Boydell's holistic viewpoint. Instead of formulating lists of core skills, behaviours and values, ICI has attempted to create an organizational framework in which employees have the space and freedom to grow as managers and as individuals.

In Chapter 7 ICI's Christopher Bull emphasizes the importance of inner and outer development and the link between personal power and effective leadership. Developing leaders, he argues, is a process of empowerment rather than simply clipping on new skills. Equally important, internal personal development needs to be harnessed in such a way as to result in positive organizational change. Linking these two areas is, Bull believes, the key to developing and utilizing individual potential.

BP's use of competences is mid-way between BA's structured yet flexible approach and ICI's holistic, open approach (Chapter 8). BP has retained some traditional elements of the competency approach such as assessment centres and generic/company-specific

lists of attributes. However, the company has moved into new
waters by incorporating a strong element of self-development into
its competency scheme.

The result of this philosophical shift is that assessment in BP has
become a less stressful and covert process. Feedback is now two-way
and is presented in such a way as to encourage managers to 'own the
data' and become committed to their own personal development.
This has enabled BP to emphasize in a positive and unthreatening
way the need for managers to adjust to change and adopt a more
open, flexible style.

Now the company is considering how to develop its assessment system further. It is considering developing job-specific
competences; identifying learning opportunities; and integrating the
assessment process with other internal management development
initiatives.

Stewart (Chapter 9) tackles an issue that has been repeatedly
referrred to by the other authors – how competency profiles can
be used against a backcloth of change and transition. Illustrating
their discussion with case-studies, they argue that competences can
be valuable assessment and development tools only if a business
recognizes that it goes through a distinct cycle of life. At each
stage of the cycle, managers need specific skills, behaviours and
management styles.

If organizations fail to understand this, they will be ill prepared
for change and transition. When this happens, they fall into the
trap of simply doing more of what was successful yesterday. This
pitfall can be avoided by looking afresh at the organization's stage
of growth and the performance criteria that are critical for present
and future performance.

Briner and Tyrrell (Chapter 10) take the debate on leadership
and team competency a step further by exploring how these two
elements are influenced by different organizational environments.
They assert that building effective teams depends on identifying the
leadership and membership competences that are most appropriate
for a particular organizational environment. All three exist in a
dynamic, flowing relationship. Like Stewart, Briner and Tyrrell
argue that, if improvements in teamwork are to be sustained, any
shifts in competences must be in tune with how the organization
is evolving.

This chapter identifies in detail the organizational environments, leadership and membership competences that form the most effective configurations. It then suggests appropriate success criteria and the way in which teamworking can be improved in each of these configurations.

In a personal account (Chapter 11), Mike O'Farrell describes how Kodak improved teamworking by concentrating on the personalities and decision-making process of managers, instead of their technical or managerial competency.

Kodak uses *action profiling*, an exercise that analyses in detail how managers view problems and formulate and implement solutions. The next step is to understand how each manager communicates this process to other team members. Other personality traits are analysed, such as personal adaptability and the ability to understand other people's points of view. These profiles enable Kodak to orientate work tasks and goals around the individual manager to a unique degree and to select teams of managers with complementary personalities and decision-making processes.

Eric Mitchell (Chapter 12) helps to round off the debate about competency by looking at a new facet – internal drive. Like Boydell and Bull, he attempts to create a developmental model that encapsulates intangible personal qualities with tangible measurable attributes. He goes on to argue that inner and outer competency are not enough to guarantee top performance. Managers also need to have the will, energy and drive to transform these competences into effective action.

Mitchell discusses a step-by-step system of analyses that helps managers to turn their vision into reality. This process identifies the personal, team and organizational implications of a vision, and includes such issues as gaining resources and creating policies and systems. Mitchell also identifies the skills needed at each stage of the analyses.

CHAPTER 6

Developing future leaders at British Airways

BRIAN O'NEILL

Education and development are necessarily future-oriented. Few of us, however, possess a crystal ball that will disclose what our future world will look like, or what must be done to fashion it. The most we can hope to do is to look at the present and the past, learn what there is to learn, and formulate a vision that must be adjusted and moulded as the future unfolds.

I would like to do just that in this chapter. I would like to tell a story about developing a profile of tomorrow's leaders and about using this profile as the basis for assessing and identifying these people. This story is part of a larger development process at British Airways which aims to identify and develop competent qualified managers and leaders. I will then attempt to draw some general points about what seems to work best in this type of assessment programme.

Developing a profile of tomorrow's leaders involves three broad issues of concern. The first is a strategic issue. What will the leaders of tomorrow look like? How can we identify in advance who they will be? Assessing who will make good leaders at some distant point in the future is difficult enough in a stable and predictable environment; it is immeasurably more difficult in a rapidly changing world.

The second issue is a technical one. What are the principal organizational conditions that must be considered and managed for such a programme to be launched? Who are the principal stakeholders, what are their interests and what are the potential conflicts of interest?

The third issue is a more speculative one. What kind of framework is required to help develop a management competence profile of leaders and managers of the future? This is one of the situations where there may be nothing as practical as a good theory. I suggest that profiling will become more effective when there are more widely agreed structures, principles and common terms. While there are no wholesale answers on the immediate horizon, perhaps we can map some of the points that will eventually lead to a suitable profiling framework.

These three areas of concern – the definition of key competences for an uncertain future, the organizational politics of implementing a leadership development programme and the need for better models – are some of the issues that deserve our closest attention. Now to move on with my story. . .

Topflight initiative at British Airways

In January 1987, British Airways embarked on an ambitious programme to develop its future leaders. At the time, chief executive Sir Colin Marshall and his top team met to chart the future course of the company. As the corporate strategy took shape, it became clear that existing management resources would be insufficient to take on the ambitious growth and expansion envisaged for the airline.

One reason for this shortage was that a significant number of managers had been lost to the company during the recession and downsizing of the early 1980s. However, by 1987, business was booming and global growth in air travel was expected to continue into the next century. Another important trend was that technology had become immensely more sophisticated and was playing an increasing part in the company's competitive position.

To meet the anticipated need for more managers, the decision was taken to implement an in-company management identification and education programme. Three management echelons were designated: the top executive level (potential directors, assistant directors), senior management (potential senior general managers), and middle managers. These programmes were collectively branded as the *Topflight Academies* to distinguish them from other newly launched initiatives offered to future managers and supervisors such as open learning programmes.

Individuals identified for the Executive Academy are placed in top-level development courses at institutions such as Harvard Business School and INSEAD. The two other echelons go through innovative, in-company educational programmes. These have been designed and developed by BA in partnership with Lancaster University. They comprise a mix of project-based learning, lectures and self-study. The Topflight Senior Management Academy leads to an MBA qualification and the Middle Management Academy to a business diploma.

I would like to emphasize that programme initiatives such as these cannot, and perhaps should not, become permanently fixed. Conditions change and experience brings new understanding of what works best. To use a popular metaphor, although the main goalposts remain firmly grounded, it makes sense from time to time to move the corner flags and renew the markings of the playing field. Such a process has been taking place at BA as the Topflight programmes have grown and evolved.

I shall now focus on the start-up period of the Topflight Programme from the spring of 1987 to the early summer of 1988. I shall also concentrate on the events leading up to the identification of the first 48 participants in the Topflight Senior Management Academy. This is perhaps an instance where it is more informative to examine a snapshot in time, rather than a moving picture that has not yet reached a conclusion.

This brings us to our first issue: how the competency profile of future senior managers was developed at BA.

Developing a profile

What is the constellation of abilities, personal qualities, values and drives that distinguish tomorrow's leader? Believing that a number of practical and useful clues can be found in management research literature, we began our search for an answer in published sources. For example we looked at the works of Boyatzis (1982), Dunnette (1971), Schroder (1986), Thornton and Byham (1982).

A second source was several internal and external psychologists who were used as assessment experts in BA. This group formed a think tank to identify what they considered as key leadership competences.

The third source, and the one that was most in tune with the life and plans of the airline, was BA's current senior managers. Individual interviews were held with 13 executive and senior managers to obtain an informed view about the strategic direction of the company; possible future scenarios; and the key leadership qualities that would ensure future success.

In the course of integrating and making sense of all this information, we found it useful to draw a distinction between 'surface' and 'source' competences. Surface competences are in 'organization speak', a language that is familiar to and readily understood by managers. We discovered seven behaviour-based, surface competences. Our experiences with other assessment programmes suggest that seven is about the number that is comfortable for assessors to handle. Source competences are more inferential in nature. They are most reliably assessed by means of thorough psychological tests and interviews. There are 15 source competences referring to intellectual effectiveness, social relationships and work approach. These two forms of competences are summarized in Table 6.1 and Table 6.2. While the distinction is by no means foolproof, surface competences appear rather more amenable to development and experience, and source competences tend to refer to qualities of the individual that are more enduring, if not immutable.

The assessment and selection process

BA designed a multiple assessment process to evaluate and select candidates who had been nominated for the programme. Four distinct perspectives were sought:

- the nominee's own view,
- his or her immediate manager's assessment,
- an informed view from a highly regarded senior manager,
- an in-depth assessment by a senior consulting psychologist.

The role of the immediate manager was largely one of counselling and mentoring. In order to underline this helping relationship, both

Table 6.1   British Airways' senior management surface competences

Vision
The ability to develop innovative, well-formed, coherent and future-oriented scenarios.

Direction
The ability to generate strategies, plans and tactics based on a good assessment of priorities, facts, risks and possibilities.

Business orientation
A business attitude and business sense that permeates every decision and action.

Results orientation
The drive to be in command, to have responsibility and achieve results and to champion worthy causes.

Managing relations
The personal qualities and interpersonal skills that promote open and constructive relations with superiors, subordinates, peers and people outside the department.

Resource management
The ability and skill to determine needs and manage the acquisition and deployment of resources, both human and physical, in a business-like way.

Large organization perspective
An appreciation of and sensitivity to the complex interdependences in a large international airline.

manager and candidate met together. This was the first formal step in the career development process. The aim of the session was to assess the candidate's current performance and his or her potential and readiness for senior general management. Another aim was to identify the most effective ways of developing the individual. This was the start of a dialogue that was expected to continue into the future. As an interview preparation aid, the manager and the candidate completed a structured questionnaire which rated performance potential and development needs.

The candidate's senior manager assessor (SMA) was selected as a credible model of sound management practice and an upholder of BA's espoused values and standards. The SMA's task was to assess the candidate's potential through a purpose-designed situational interview. This is a fairly powerful tool consisting of several descriptions

Table 6.2 British Airways' senior management source competences

---

Intellectual effectiveness
- critical analytical thinking
- synthesis
- conceptual thinking
- original and divergent thinking
- flexibility of thinking
- balanced thinking

Relationship with others
- social impact
- interdependence
- managing upward relations
- managing downward relations
- managing other relations

Work approach
- judgement
- decisiveness
- effectiveness, drive
- energy and stamina

---

of true-to-life problems that a senior general manager at BA might encounter. The candidate is instructed to adopt the role of senior general manager and explain how he or she would handle each situation. The SMA records the responses verbatim and subsequently scores them against the surface competences.

The psychological assessment closely resembles the in-depth assessment that is usually conducted with BA's senior management candidates. This consists of an extensive battery of ability tests and personality questionnaires, followed by a one-to-one interview with a psychologist. For the academy, the psychological report is structured around the source competences.

The final stage in the process, and the most valuable one for the purposes of selection, was an integration conference held by the SMA and the psychologist to share, debate and distil their respective findings. This yielded an overall rating of potential, as well as ratings on each of the seven surface competences: vision; direction; results orientation; business orientation; managing relations; resource management; and large organization perspective.

These integrated findings, together with a written recommendation for career placement and development, were then reviewed by a board of senior manager assessors under the chairmanship of the director of human resources. Their decisions were then announced to the nominees, their managers and their directors.

As a fitting finale to the process, grand plans were laid for a four-corner feedback conference with the candidate, the immediate manager, the SMA and the psychologist. All would actively participate in pulling together the various strands of the assessment, exploring their relevance and implications for the individual's career and providing a foundation for developmental planning and action. In the event, it rarely happened like that. The logistical difficulties involved in bringing together the four parties at a single time and place proved to be almost insurmountable. Feedback usually took place but rarely with more than one of the three assessors available to the candidate at any one session.

Lessons learned

What are the learning points from this one assessment programme conducted in a brief snapshot in time? Let us return to the three original issues: defining tomorrow's leaders; the tactical issues that arise when such a development programme is launched; and the organizational framework that is required to develop competency profiles.

Competence and strategy

I believe there is more art than science in divining a profile of leadership competences that will make sense in a few years from now. Certainly there is a wealth of useful published research on which to draw. We can have a high degree of confidence, for instance, in the generalization that successful leaders are people who think analytically and understand things conceptually. Certain personality measures, such as ascendancy and sociability, have also been found to predict accurately managerial effectiveness.

But in the end, profiles that are founded on past research alone are backward-looking at best. They may well miss or underestimate competences that are important now, or will be important in the future. Ideally, then, the leadership profile should also be grounded in a vision of the future. This should be a vision derived from long-term forecasts and an exhaustive analysis of the geo-political environment; market trends and possible discontinuities; a long-term corporate strategy and so on. For instance, enough was probably known several years ago to anticipate the international dimension that is now so important in today's leadership and that should arguably be embedded now in current profiles and development programmes.

Proactive profiling, if I can call it that, is obviously most easily accomplished in organizations and industries that have greatest control over their future. It is also helpful to have stable and predictable social environments. In these circumstances, it is profitable as a part of the strategic planning function. But what of companies and industries that regularly confront less stable conditions? Companies can be immensely sensitive to these uncertain conditions. For example, airlines face the normal course of economic events, such as oil prices and currency exchange rates. However they must also cope with major crises, such as the Chernobyl disaster and the Libyan affair, which can have grave effects on international air travel and revenues. Quite clearly, proactive profiling is not the complete answer.

Indeed, it might be argued that the world is changing in so many respects and at such a rate that any future-based profile for almost any industry will become dated long before its current applications will bear fruit. I am not sure if there can be a definitive response to this argument, but it does underline the need for leaders who are able to handle uncertainty and manage change effectively. It also supports the need to build a high degree of flexibility into the design of management profiles and development programmes.

Several provisions were made in these respects in the BA profiling exercise. First, the company acknowledged that profiles needed to change and adjust depending on what the future may bring. They are not etched in stone. Secondly, candidates were expected to have a certain 'dispositional flexibility' which included an aptitude for dealing with uncertainty and an inclination and ability to handle complexity. A natural curiosity and an interest in ongoing learning were also favoured together with the corresponding intellectual abilities. Thirdly, a principle of 'competency compensation' was applied. This recognized that not everyone, or indeed anyone, was expected to measure up in every respect to the idealized profiles. In considering a candidate's potential, therefore, assessors and psychologists pay careful consideration to how an individual's strengths in some particular competences compensate for manifest weaknesses in others. Heterogeneity rather than a cloning of competence was considered more adaptive for the growing of a well-rounded leadership.

Tactical issues

Tactical issues involved in the implementation of an in-company management assessment and development programme will vary from company to company, depending on a number of factors. These include the organizational structure; its history and reputation in career development; the relative emphasis on operational versus strategic priorities; pressures from the City and so on. But there are probably a handful that are important and common enough to consider in this general forum. These include the following tactical issues.

SHORT-TERM VERSUS LONG-TERM PERSPECTIVE

An extended and systematic management development programme is only for organizations with an eye to the long-term future and that are prepared to make a heavy investment in that future. But even with such a commitment, there will be pressure from the City to weight priorities more heavily in favour of short-term profitability. Expecting senior managers to spend time selecting future leaders when faced with poor quarterly figures is tantamount in their eyes to fiddling while the corporate city burns. This is clearly an issue where intervention from the chief executive is very important.

Applying a longer time perspective to management education may be less important for businesses that are able to go out to the market place and simply 'buy' senior managers as and when required. But even this seems a risky option as the current signs point to a future problem with the supply of managers.

CORPORATE VERSUS DEPARTMENTAL INTERESTS

One of the anticipated issues at BA was the conflict between corporate and departmental needs and interests. Traditionally, the airline has been strongly departmentalized. Many of the larger departments, such as engineering and flight operations, are organized along specialist lines and have proved to be relatively impermeable to outsiders. While much of this organizational 'smokestacking' has its origins in genuine occupational differences and legitimate legal restrictions, parochial attitudes had tended to evolve over the years. These were seen as dysfunctional to the harmonious operation of the airline as a whole.

In the event, this obstacle proved less of a problem than anticipated. Few managers took issue with the Topflight Academy's aim to create talent pools as a primary source of future leaders. They recognized that it made good sense for both the company and the programme participant.

To a large extent, this positive response speaks well of the breadth and maturity of the managers concerned. It also highlights the enormous importance of communication which took place through presentations, hand-outs, brochures and *ad hoc* discussions. Start-up presentations to potential participants and their immediate managers were also held as a two-way dialogue to allow their views, anxieties and queries to be tabled and answered. Even more extensive discussions were held before and after the assessments with groups of senior manager assessors. And, to close the loop, a questionnaire survey was conducted at the end of the first cycle to determine what had or had not worked for the different groups.

A further measure confirmed the non-partisan nature of the initiative and underlined its high corporate profile. This was the selection of highly credible and respected men and women as senior manager assessors. These individuals were deliberately assigned to candidates from different departments. An engineering candidate, for instance, might be assessed by a top manager from marketing. These SMAs effectively became the champions of the initiative in their own departments.

SPECIALISTS VERSUS GENERALISTS

Many of the potential candidates for the Senior Management Programme were and are specialized by occupation and by experience. Many know about their own 'smokestack' only. In some cases, they may know about only a limited part of their field. This, I assume, mirrors the experience of many other sectors such as information technology and financial services.

Although many very capable engineers and pilots joined the programme, the specialist was often difficult to assess and develop. On the one hand, it is extremely difficult to estimate a candidate's potential for general management when he or she has had little or no experience in any of the broad areas of people management, operational management, sales and revenue generation. On the other hand, if a specialist has been positively assessed, how does he or she catch up in a demanding MBA programme while holding down a responsible job?

Neat solutions are not easily found to these issues. In practice, the assessors made every effort to discern proof of potential by paying special attention to the evidence for 'source competence' and by making allowances for limited experience. In many cases, the assessment team strongly recommended that a specialist make a lateral move into another department as a means of catching up on missing experience. In many other cases, specialists were encouraged to resubmit their nomination at a later date.

Despite these efforts, the disproportionate number of specialist candidates who were not nominated proved discouraging in the extreme to their managers and peers. Naturally, this has done little for the overall public view of the programme or for the willingness of others to put their heads on the block. BA is now considering undertaking measures to provide pre-programme preparation for specialists. However, the issue may be too fundamental to be wholly resolved in this manner.

What seems to be at stake here are questions of standards and method. Is it reasonable to impose an absolute standard of competence in a company that is playing 'catch-up' in its management development activities? Is it realistic to attempt to predict which pilots, engineers and IT specialists will make future leaders when many have yet to be exposed to the most fundamental management experiences?

Current expert opinion would advise a religious application of absolute standards of competence using situational interviews, assessment centres and other real-life simulations of the management experience. I am less sure that this is the way to progress. In the first place, even the best management profile makes a shaky foundation for absolute standards, resting as it does on speculative ground. Secondly, the demand for managers is likely to exceed the available supply. Given the less than perfect hit rate expected from even the most rigorous and reliable assessment methods, it would seem more sensible to apply standards flexibly rather than rigidly. It would seem wise to defer selection decisions until as late a point in the process as possible. Initially, methods should be used that do not discriminate against people who lack broad management experience.

What does this mean in practice? It probably means using 'softer' measures of suitability. These should be based more on self-assessment and assessment of source competence rather than surface competence. British Airways is currently going some way in that direction. This probably also means taking a greater risk with the expenditure of development resources – there will be a risk of a lower success rate as more people will be selected into development programmes based on less 'hard' evidence. Although this must surely entail some lost development opportunity, it also means that a greater absolute number of managers and leaders are developed. Even those who do not complete the programme will benefit. This will mean fewer dissatisfied stakeholders.

SELECTION FOR DEVELOPMENT VERSUS POSITION

From time to time, a dilemma arose in the evaluation of the assessment data. A candidate might appear to be a future leader but be deemed unlikely material for the academic rigours of a university postgraduate degree. Alternatively, he or she might have high potential for the MBA but be seen to be fatally flawed for the senior management role. Hopefully, business and academia are progressing towards an equitable and sensible resolution that accommodates their own respective interests as well as those of the individual candidate.

Recognizing individual differences in learning styles and temperament, business would do well to make provision for alternative routes into senior positions. Some individuals will benefit from the

MBA, while others should have opportunities to develop and rise in other more experiential ways. University business faculties, on the other hand, would do equally well to examine the logic of selection processes that may be unfairly biased in favour of scholastic ability at the cost of more practical managerial abilities. Clearly, one of the tasks here is to devise more reliable and better-balanced measures of ability and aptitude that will be of service to all parties.

Until this issue is resolved, we can expect some degree of tension and uncertainty.

RESOURCE CONSTRAINTS

A development programme of this magnitude cannot be undertaken lightly. It demands the budgeting and dedication of time, people and other resources. It is not an activity that can be covered by normal slack. Freeing up staff and line managers to participate is going to be more of a problem for companies that have cut back on their management structures in these lean and mean post-recession days. It is also going to be a problem for an organization experiencing one of those cataclysmic and usually unanticipated events – the kind that takes precedence over everything else and stops other developments dead in their tracts; in short, a special organizational application of Murphy's Law.

Our particular cataclysmic event was the merging of British Airways with British Caledonian. Murphy had a field day. In view of the overwhelming demands this placed on senior management resources, the assessment programme was quickly and understandably relegated to the background until more propitious times. In fact, there were few periods during the first assessment–feedback cycle when some cancellation or rescheduling was not required. This did nothing for the credibility of the programme. It created considerable dissatisfaction with 'the administration process' among many of the candidates, immediate managers and other stakeholders.

Clearly there is no ready answer to a 'Murphy event' in the great cosmic scheme. I would say to companies frequently visited by such events: 'Design maximum flexibility into the process and keep communicating status to those most affected – the candidates.'

Looking back at those ever-changing days of 1987, I have been tempted to alter a long-held principle that the primary responsibility for the assessment of future senior managers rests with current senior managers. Making selection decisions for high-level promotion and development is a grave management responsibility that has long-lasting effects on individual lives and the success of the company; hence the use of senior managers in the role of Topflight assessors. But if management resources cannot be spared, or if they must be held in reserve (so to speak) for the cataclysmic event, alternative approaches to assessment must be sought.

There may be a case here for looking outside the organization for resources. Given that the competency profile and the assessment process have been defined and approved by the top executive, perhaps it makes sense to delegate the assessment responsibility to professionals who are appropriately skilled and who have a broader perspective on management selection issues. Combining this external assessment with the immediate manager's assessment and the individual's own self-evaluation may well supply the data necessary for a sound decision. The role of the corporate manager would then be a relatively straightforward one of selection. This option makes even more sense if it is decided that source competences will carry the burden of the assessment.

PERSONAL STAKES AND INTERESTS

Until now our discussion has been largely at a global level, with little reference to the individuals most directly and personally affected by a corporate intervention into career development. These were the immediate managers, those who were or were not nominated and those who were and were not selected. How were these people affected?

The managers of potential participants very quickly caught on to what the programme was letting their best subordinate managers in for. Time spent in study and course work would be time lost from work objectives. They, the immediate managers, stood to lose their most prized protégés without any *quid pro quo*. Should their nominee be unsuccessful, they could well be left with a dissatisfied subordinate and a counselling problem to boot. Some were also concerned about their own reputation, should their nominee fail to be selected.

85

While many of their fears were realized, the immediate managers were generally found to be an important and supportive resource to both the programme and the individual. Again, with the near perfect vision of hindsight, I believe that more can and should be made of this resource. Training and workshops could help managers to nominate and counsel more effectively, and to integrate their career counselling role with that of performance appraisal. Immediate managers, moreover, should be rewarded and not penalized for grooming and nominating young talent. Why not create a resource bank of mature experienced managers who are approaching retirement who can be a useful resource to successful nominators?

Every potential nominee and participant stood to win or lose a great deal: the stakes range from the grand prize of a place on the Academy leading to an MBA to an unjust and unwarranted reputation as one of the 'also-rans' in what is sometimes seen as the only race in town. But even with the first prize there was something of a Catch 22. Participants were expected to stay in their present positions for the duration of their two-year programme. Given the pressures of the Academy on their time and personal resources, promotion to senior management position was thought to be excessively demanding.

In accord with the programme's objective of growing generalists, once participants were formally qualified, they were expected to step outside their specialities and departments and accept appointments elsewhere. Selection to the Academy, in short, could carry quite a price tag for the ambitious man or woman who had mapped out a vertical career path in the department of his or her choice.

In the event, many of these expectations of programme participants have been considerably modified. Indeed, several of the first 48 candidates had already been promoted to senior positions before the course had begun.

There seem to be no obvious solutions to these legitimate but conflicting interests. How does an organization protect its fledgling leaders until maturity is reached? How does it grow broad-based all-round managers who understand the complexities of an airline, when many high-flyers want a more restricted vista? What will motivate the manager-in-development to sacrifice high promotion while less endowed individuals are receiving their senior wings?

Perhaps the answers lie with the management levels towards

which programmes like the Senior Management Academy are targeted. Perhaps fewer conflicts would arise if participants were selected from junior and senior rather than middle management ranks. Juniors would still be far enough removed from the senior promotion stakes and the seasoned seniors would have arrived already. There would be a stable period for learning and consolidation. But this too has a downside: juniors would be too inexperienced to take full advantage of the development experience and middle managers would, of course, miss out.

Yet another solution might be to delay implementation until other high quality programmes are developed for those who, for whatever reason, were not selected onto the programme. Certainly, several of the senior manager assessors felt the need to have something substantive and useful to offer all candidates, including those not selected.

It is probably impossible to implement such a large-scale programme for future senior managers without gaps and strains of this sort. Perhaps it is necessary and more efficient to work things out in an ongoing way as the programme evolves and the various issues take shape. But the issues outlined in this section seem to be the ones that were most in need of clear policy directives from the outset. Launching a successful programme demands the prior establishment of some fundamental rules of the game, rules that are endorsed unequivocally by the executive directors and are disseminated to all potential players.

A framework for profiling competence

Despite the advantages and the many applications of competency profiling, there is a surprising shortage of theoretical frameworks to guide the practitioner and researcher. In the British Airways project, we felt seriously handicapped by this problem.

The lack of a generic model of management competence may be partly explained by a mistaken belief that competences are unique and specific to particular applications, organizations, times and places and that, being infinitely variable, they are not therefore amenable to generalization. The work of Boyatzis, Schroder and other researchers and practitioners indicates that this is not the case. Competences are generally applicable across organizations and similar positions.

As a stimulus to further thought, it might be helpful to consider here some of the characteristics of an overall framework for management competence profiling. I make an assumption that such a framework would include a listing of critical competence definitions, arranged in an organized structure that supported the following characteristics:

- This framework would be capable of representing management competences for different types of organizations and at different stages of an organization's evolution.
- It would be comprehensive enough to describe any management position, excluding specific technical skills and knowledge.
- It would be capable of describing and doing justice to the individual's competences. While it may be too much to expect a portrait of the whole dynamic person, it would capture his or her key strengths and weaknesses.
- It would incorporate management competences that have been shown to be related to successful management performance, or to be otherwise useful for assessment or development.
- It would provide some reasonable base for determining the extent to which a competence is trainable or amenable to development and the extent, correspondingly, of its immutability.
- It would provide guidelines on how a strength in one particular competence might compensate for a weakness in another. Indeed competence compensation could be within an individual or a group.
- It would be expressed in terms that are readily understood and agreed. Each of the constituent competences therefore would have clearly defined behavioural indicators.

Conclusion

Profiles and programmes such as those I have described are conceived and given birth at a specific time and in a specific corporate environment. This environment has its own history, its own character and its own culture. Competence profiles, therefore, must mirror and reflect the parent organization's perceptions of its own realities and values.

However, like all offspring, competences can also revitalize an ageing parent by challenging the status quo. They can anticipate the future and not simply follow the past. Ideally, an organization's leadership profile should inspire change and growth.

A profile can also be seen as an important interface linking members to their corporate organization. It represents and projects the qualities prized by the organization as goals of excellence for individual aspiration and development.

The profile competences themselves are sometimes seen as the elementary building blocks and linkages between the various sub-systems of human resource management: selection; development; performance appraisal; career and succession planning; skill inventories. In this respect, they provide a useful common language for the members of the organization.

As we approach the next decade I believe that management profiling will become an altogether more sophisticated and systematic process. The profiles themselves will become an even more useful tool in the task of selecting and developing tomorrow's leader.

References

Boyatzis, R. (1982), *The Competent Manager* (New York: Wiley).

Dunnette, M. D. (1971), 'The assessment of managerial talent', in Paul McReynolds (ed.), *Advances in Psychological Assessment* Vol. 2 (Palo Alto, Calif.: Science and Behaviour Books).

Schroder, H. M. (1986), 'Managerial competence and style', unpublished paper (University of Florida).

Thornton, G. C. and Byham, W. C. (1982), *Assessment Centres and Management Performance* (New York: Academic Press).

CHAPTER 7

Releasing of power in ICI

CHRISTOPHER BULL

This chapter tells the story of introducing people in ICI to new and challenging concepts in the area of human functioning, power and leadership.

The story starts with the relationship between myself and Robin Eades, of ICI, and our commitment to each other's development. It has grown from this point to involve many other people and various major commercial enterprises.

Four main sections will be examined:

- the basic philosophy behind the work that was carried out in ICI;
- the way the work was carried out, focusing particularly on the way we worked with people and with the organization;
- the results so far;
- the next steps needed to encourage further developments.

Basic philosophy

When associated with any development activity that involves people, it is a good idea to have a reasonably clear notion of what we are dealing with. If we are not clear about this to start with, or at least clear about our assumptions, it is likely to lead us into tricky water at a later stage. It is like a development chemist who is unclear about the nature of the materials he is using to produce a new reaction – it could provide some surprising and devastating results! When working with large business communities, extreme and unexpected results are not very welcome and are often the precursor to the cessation of development work. Therefore, as a guide to our practice, we make some assumptions about the nature of humans and organizations and the way they function and malfunction.

We assume that the inherent nature of people is good. In their natural state, men and women are intelligent, able, curious, energetic and collaborative. Any characteristics that are not positive are conditioned by unprocessed negative experiences that have occurred in their lives. This does not mean that we predict that all humans will function 'fully humanly'. On the whole, we expect that their conditioning will lead to all sorts of inappropriate behaviour, upset and uproar when they are under pressure. We do assume, however, that the potential to act humanly, and thereby function well, exists in all healthy humans.

This makes the task of creating leaders an interesting proposition. Often leadership development has made the assumption that people need to add skills to their repertoire in order to gain something extra that transforms them into leaders. We do not agree with this idea and view it as one way in which so-called leaders subconsciously maintain control in the name of leadership. We believe that everyone is a leader. Men and women have the potential to develop themselves and others into fully functioning people who are able to think, decide, act powerfully and lead others to do the same.

It is probably obvious that the way I am using some household terms here is not conventional and I will, therefore, attempt to define them.

First, leadership is the ability to create environments where people can be appropriately human. This means that people are functioning well, they are clear about goals, directions and processes and they are able to adapt to changing circumstances quickly and accurately. They will also be able to assist others to do the same.

'Power' is the ability to create, sustain and nurture life. What many people mean by the word 'power' could be more accurately described as *control*. This urge to control comes from conditioning,

91

which was originally instilled by fear, manipulation and humiliation. Power in our terms is the ability to assist people to deal with this conditioning in a productive way and to base their decisions and actions on the thinking that occurs when they are connected to their inherent nature.

Thus developing leaders is a process of empowerment. Although this power is inherent, people need assistance to release it, rather than to acquire some new external skills, attitudes and abilities. An integral aspect of expressing natural power is to help managers to release *their* abilities to assist *others* to release their power. We would contend that the core process of leadership is creating leaders.

To summarize our assumptions:

- all men and women are leaders;
- people are inherently powerful and have the ability to express this benignly;
- the task of developing leaders is the task of releasing their inherent power and assisting others to do the same.

Given that these assumptions about humans guide our practice, we need also to formulate and clarify our assumptions about organizations.

It was not until recently that we realized that a business organization is, in essence, a commercial community – a collection of people working together to achieve certain commercial goals. This realization enabled us to assume that everyone involved wanted the community to succeed. In a way, the organization's ability to function shows how flexible its people really are.

We assumed that the organization's form and practices evolved from energy coming from two basic sources: people's inherent nature and conditioned reactions. Some forms and processes would be rational and support any intervention that attempted to increase the incidence of human leadership. However, some forms and processes would be reacting against this leadership thrust. These opposite impulses would inevitably affect our work. Some individuals would attack us, while some would see us or our process as the answer to everything. We knew that all these distorted views would have to be dealt with humanly and decisively and would provide the fuel for the continued developmental work.

Another consideration was the difficulty that is commonly reported in the transfer of learning. The key problem is that the safety that enables people to release their power during a training workshop is not available when they return to work. We wanted to try to develop a way of working that would enable access to the culture that is created in training workshops. We assumed that the workplace culture discourages learning but encourages, albeit unconsciously, 'no mistakes'. We also assumed that human beings are constantly developing, whatever the culture, but that the culture will affect the *rate* of development. In a sense, people naturally try to develop their ability to function humanly all the time, whatever the conditions, even if it looks (or feels) very different to this. Access to a culture that supports this urge will enhance the development process.

Another element we wanted to cater for was the connection between internal personal development and the creation of change. We wanted to build a link between the development of each individual and the changes they wanted to develop in their workplace or other sectors of their lives. This is key in institutionalizing the development process. We did not wish to spend our energies developing some very aware people who did not have a positive and practical impact on their situations. Indeed, we see the two fields of activity – internal development and external action – as essential to accelerating the enhancement of full human functioning.

To summarize our assumptions about organizations:

- organizations are human communities,
- they have been, and are, influenced by conditioned human drives,
- safe spaces need to be created if people are to learn and grow in the existing organizational culture,
- for people to develop fully as leaders, internal development and external change are necessary.

What we did

We decided that our thinking and assumptions needed to be shared with any potential participants before becoming involved in the ICI development programme. Given our stance about the inherent nature of human beings, we wanted to make sure that the people who attended the workshops really wanted to be there and made their own decision about attending. We therefore ran a half-day introductory session and gave people as much information as possible about the programme.

We then organized a series of workshops, each separated by about six to eight weeks, to help tackle the problem of learning transfer. We assumed that people would not necessarily have an accurate or complete diagnosis about themselves or their situations. Returning to their place of engagement and trying to apply what they had learned after each workshop would reveal where the diagnosis was inaccurate or incomplete. This could be dealt with at the next workshop.

We decided that each workshop should have a key theme and that these themes would become progressively more stretching. We designed the following events:

Workshop 1   This introduces participants to a simple, yet powerful, social planning process that they use with each other to identify the current situation and develop a vision and key directions. They then set short-, medium- and long-term goals. The workshop also initiates and develops the groups that support the process back in the workplace.

Workshop 2   This introduces to participants the process of coun-selling each other to deal with the conditioning that naturally arises as they implement their goals.

Workshop 3   This refines the counselling skills and introduces new ideas and approaches in the areas of building relationships and networks.

We wanted to ensure that participants developed strong connec-tions with each other and were able to use these connections at work. To achieve this, small support groups were formed during the first workshop which were to last through the whole programme of three workshops. The groups were encouraged to meet at least once during the period between each workshop. By doing this we saw ourselves acting against the organizational norm of isolation which, in our opinion, causes much pain, disruptive action and irrational behaviour.

The basic approach was to create a series of spaces in which individuals could connect to their own and each other's humanity and become clear about their respective situations and goals. We also tried to assist them to continue this connection at work, thereby enabling each of them to use their natural intelligence effectively in any situation they encountered.

We did not make a big fuss about what we were doing. We had noticed in earlier work that development seems to progress well and naturally when people are involved in it on a one-to-one contact basis. To make a start, ICI's internal consultant identified who he thought would benefit from the programme. These people were invited to the introductory session to make their own judgements about the programme's suitability.

The first series of workshops was run in 1985 and five have been run since then. After the first workshop, it became evident that the participants had benefited a great deal. They were very keen to be connected with each other and to continue to use the planning, counselling and networking processes. This led us to build a network of people who had attended the programmes. We also decided to build a small group of people who would be developed as co-trainers and consultants for future programmes, as well as in other initiatives which used the same basic approaches.

The developments that arose from our original initiative include the following:

- a training programme that helps leaders develop themselves and other leaders;
- a series of support groups, which enable people to build supportive and challenging relationships, which can meet at the workplace and continue the process;
- a small group of increasingly skilled and able line manager consultants, which increases the leadership pool for this specific developmental process;

- the core of a network of people who can build high levels of trust very quickly, learn and use new theory and practice, and build new support groups where necessary.

The results

In general we can say that people have taken to this approach like ducks to water. Although the first workshop of the first programme was a little stormy, since then people who have come to the programmes have usually been recommended by others, so any storms have been small, contained and well used.

People tackle a variety of issues in their situations, both in their homes and at the workplace. One example is of a participant who was very keen to become closer to his son. He decided to pay his son as much attention as possible when he was with him to see what results he got. He was very pleased when his son increasingly wanted to be with him and became visibly brighter and attentive. For the first time in his life, his son did not want him to go to work but wanted him to stay and be with him. However, the manager also realized that *his* father had not spent much time with him. The resulting conditioning was affecting his life and, in particular, his relationships with other men. He was able to work on minimizing the effects of this in his support group. This in turn enabled him to build closer and more trusting relationships with his colleagues at work which, he estimates, have resulted in a considerable improvement in business performance.

Another example is of a participant who left the first workshop full of resolve to tackle his indecisive boss. His strategy was to pay extra attention to his boss when he was facing a problem. He then used with his boss one of the workshop processes of creating a vision of how an issue could be resolved, setting long-term goals in the light of the vision, then working back from the long-term goals to the present day. This process placed his boss in a novel position – he was faced with a decision, he wanted the long-term goals and vision, he had been given unconditional attention. The boss made the decision. It was not the decision his subordinate wanted but it *was* a decision, which was his prime objective. The fact that it was not the decision that the subordinate wanted gave him some grist for the mill to work on his support group!

96

In order to gain a wider picture of the programme's impact, we arranged preliminary interviews with prospective participants and their bosses and then follow-up interviews with them after the programme. Data from these interviews indicated that participants gained the following:

- 'increased confidence';
- 'increased ability to examine all aspects of a situation before making a decision and acting on it';
- 'an ability to "counsel" people while discussing day-to-day subjects and work issues';
- 'more skill and ability to design strategy, set and implement goals';
- 'improved ability to increase other people's confidence in themselves and their ability to lead in their own situations';
- 'ability to do in a more relaxed way things I know should be done but don't want to do';
- 'more ability and confidence to talk in public and run meetings well';
- 'more able to manage myself and really have a good time';
- 'increased flexibility in the way I do my work and enable others to do theirs!'

The majority of support groups that were formed during the programmes are still meeting. Some new ones have been formed that make more sense geographically or from the point of view of bringing people together at similar stages of their development. Some support groups have been integrated into the workplace. For example, three men who work on the same corridor get together weekly to examine their business activities for the week and to plan their next steps. The helpful thing about the support group culture is that it is safe and therefore the people in it can deal with the *reality* of their situation.

We have had about four network meetings with reasonable attendance. The different programme populations have mixed very well and very quickly. The network meetings generally last about a day. People spend about half the time in support groups and the other half learning and experimenting with new and different approaches to developing leadership.

We have built an excellent core leadership group which meets about once every six weeks for about half a day. The group has a mix of participants from the programmes and members have increased their ability to use and apply the thinking that they originally learned on the programme. In addition, we include members of the core leadership group in the staff teams of the programmes. This has accelerated their development, provided a good link for the participants and developed internal resources to run the programme.

Unfortunately, as the people in the core leadership group developed, some were promoted, moved location or obtained 'better' jobs outside the company. This has obviously been very good for them as individuals and also productive for the company but it means the core leadership group constantly changes. This provides us with an additional challenge which we are currently addressing.

Internal consultancy work has also flowed from the work we have done. We are now working with three business units within the company, using the same basic approach but adjusting it to the particular circumstances of each unit. One unit has a world-wide business with a turnover in excess of £500 million, another is a new business that is growing at a phenomenal rate and the other is an expanding trading company.

Next steps

Our intention is to move forward on the following fronts:

- continuing work with ICI's business units to institutionalize the approach to releasing people's leadership;
- continuing developing the core leadership group and involving them in the running of programmes, network events and internal consultancy work;
- offering two full programmes per year within ICI;
- supporting past participants in transferring the new ways of working to their businesses.

With the resources that have been developed, we are now in a position to continue the programmes and increase the work that has arisen with the business units. Obviously the two types of 'intervention' will feed each other and the network of people using similar approaches will grow.

References

Bull, C. and Mills, (1981), 'An open systems approach', in Nixon, B. *New Approaches to Management Development*, (Aldershot: Gower).
Bull, C. (1988), 'Leadership – A search for new meaning, unpublished paper.
Jackins, H. (1983), *The Reclaiming of Power* (Rational Island).

CHAPTER 8

BP's move from assessment to development

JULIAN GREATREX*

In 1987 I took over the corporate assessment boards run by the BP Group, which primarily acted as filters for the high-flyer system run by the organization. One of the first questions I asked was, 'What's in it for the individual, particularly those not "selected"?' The second question I asked was, 'On what criteria are people being assessed? How relevant are these criteria to the individual and the organization?'

These two questions reflect some of my key working assumptions, which mostly centre around valuing development as a 'core process', both for individuals and organizations, and managing change effectively, both personal and organizational. Moreover, I believe that people must own the data and therefore have full access to it.

Out of these values and assumptions, which are increasingly shared around the BP Group, came the vision to shift our approach from assessment to development. This requires us to move from:

* secrecy to openness
* one-way to two-way feedback
* stress to personal change and transition.

In order to understand these points fully, I need to explain a little more about the history of the assessment boards. These have existed in BP for the last 12 years and have always worked on a fairly formal

---

* I am very grateful to Peter Phillips for his help in preparing this paper.

level. This approach tended to be part of a 'black box' syndrome on management development. It paid lip service to the notion of self-development, but was much more concerned in reality with organizational assessment of potential. This is, of course, the typical background to many existing assessment centres.

My intention here is to outline, as a practitioner, the steps we took to move the emphasis from assessment to development; to show the key role of core competences in the process; and to indicate what further steps still need to be taken. As such, I am outlining a very practical piece of action research.

Propositions

A major constraint facing us was that assessments boards were clearly part of people's perceptions. It would be much cleaner if you could start from scratch (to quote the vernacular, there would be less 'contamination') but life isn't like that.

Given this constraint, we were still able to make the following statements:

- assessment for assessment's sake is not functional either for the individual or the organization (especially the individual);
- solely relying on assessment leads to a heavy dependence on motivating people through money (extrinsic motivation);
- a development focus is required as a motivational tool: through self-assessment people will own the data and their commitment will be obtained in the form of intrinsic motivation.

Research evidence, obtained from within BP, gave some very definite indicators of the ways in which individual perceptions and attitudes were changing. Examples include:

* a more open culture in which expectations are exchanged and negotiated and where the contract is 'two-way';
* an increasing acceptance of the value of managerial career-anchors and professional/technical career-anchors, coupled with a need for parallel career structures;

101

* an increasing acceptance of the value of such concepts as self-actualization (reflected in self-development) and that such a proactive stance is being rewarded by the organization.

These changes must be set against some quite profound organizational changes since 1987, which also give a taste for what can be increasingly expected in the future. These organizational changes include:

* increasingly complex organizational structures and the need for people to manage ambiguity and complex boundaries;
* an increasing trend towards internationalization, partly through acquisition (e.g. BP America, Britoil) and the need to develop people to manage effectively different national and organizational cultures and to think more strategically;
* a move towards a more market-oriented, client-centred organizational culture and the changes in philosophy and approach required, for example in technical services functions;
* 'delayering' of management structures so that accountability is increasingly devolved, requiring more business management and an entrepreneurial approach;
* the need to develop a more flexible, open management style in order to manage these organizational changes more effectively.

Taking these points as the backdrop, we now need to outline the research process that helped us to achieve the following steps:

(1) identify the *core competences* required for managerial effectiveness now and in the future;
(2) map out the *developmental suggestions*;
(3) get all parties involved and owning the *process*.

Core competences

Using various methodologies such as Critical Incident and Repertory Grid, we went through a process of job analysis. We did this by asking approximately 30 senior managers to identify which key *behaviours* they associated with effective and ineffective managerial

102

performance. Unsurprisingly, extensive data were collected which were then analysed and clustered so as to get a *classification system* that was coherent, had face validity and could be used operationally. I accept some people's reservations about the dangers of 'contaminated' samples and the risk of cloning, etc. However, the reality of organizational change is somewhat different from pure research – and that can also be rather spurious as everyone knows!

What emerged was a mixture of concrete behaviours, sets of values and beliefs that together give a very powerful picture of the corporate culture of a large multinational organization. These clusters included:

* achievement motivation
* interpersonal skills
* cognitive skills
* flexibility.

These can be expressed as a *pawnbroker model* (see Figure 8.1).

If I relate this model to the organizational changes at BP, the following key requirements emerge for managers of the future.

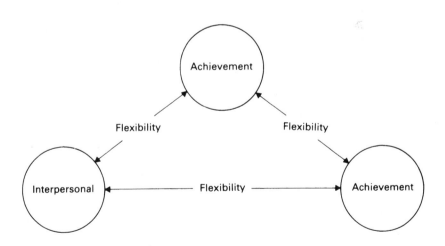

Figure 8.1 Pawnbroker model of competences

These are:

- strategic leadership
- business management
- flexible management styles.

These requirements formed the basis of the new rating system which began operating in 1988 on our development and assessment boards (DABs).

DABs use the following assessment methods:

(1) Assessment of individuals in group and in one-to-one situations, using the core competences framework. Individuals also assess themselves. Some limited feedback is given at this stage.

(2) Psychometric tests, such as a range of ability tests and Occupational Personality Questionnaire (OPQ).

(3) Individual exercises.

(4) Integration exercises, where data are brought together for each individual to exercise his or her business judgement.

(5) Feedback of results, where I myself act as facilitator/career counsellor. I also discuss the implications of this feedback in terms of training, development and overall career and personal development. There is a particularly strong focus on self-development.

(6) Discussions with general managers to discuss the implications of the feedback, such as potential career tracks.

If you actually compare BP's core competences (see appendix) with other classification systems (e.g. Boyatzis and Schroder) or with related instruments such as the OPQ, there is fundamentally no difference except for one crucial point. This is that the behaviours listed are cultural artifacts of the BP organization – what the company means by commercial judgement is what is registered by managers. Therefore, the utility of this is high within BP but limited elsewhere.

One other point that will require further work is whether any weighting of these clusters can be discerned. Based on some preliminary research work by BP, it seems clear that assessors have tended to rate achievement, motivation and cognitive skills higher than interpersonal sensitivity. This may be a function of both the organization culture and the covert thought that interpersonal skills are perhaps more 'developable' than the other qualities.

There are a lot of pointers for further work in this area, but for the moment let me stress the way these core competences are also being used in specific areas such as appraisal, recruitment and training. Clearly, they have the potential to form a basic building block for the management development policies of an organization.

Development

The chief area for further work is development, particularly self-development. To achieve this we have to incorporate a much larger element of self-assessment and ensure that all the 'data' are available. Another step, which is often overlooked, is the need to set up a process that will facilitate individual development.

As BP's 'research project' developed, it became apparent that it needed to go through several stages – first identifying the core competences, then getting them to work in operational settings such as development and assessment boards, then picking up the developmental implications. But running through all this has been the need to manage the process so that the key parties remain involved and committed. What we have been carrying out is, of course, action research.

As regards the development focus, there have been certain crucial, symbolic actions – such as ensuring that the word 'development' is more upfront. More importantly, specific steps have been taken with individual managers. These steps include the following:

- Managers assess themselves against the core competences. This makes the competences public, whereas before they were part of the 'black box' associated with high-flyer management development.
- Feedback of results has become much more complete and extensive, and in many ways more challenging to the individual. The trick for people such as myself is to help people to 'own the data' and then to help them to start thinking about what to do next. They need to consider their personal development within that and any particular training that may be of help.
- Managers use ensuing discussions with their general manager and other mentor-type figures as a springboard for managing

their own development effectively (but in an interdependent rather than dependent way). These discussions are built into the whole process and are vital in terms of people recognizing the organizational legitimacy and priority attached to this activity.

Further steps

Finally, it would be useful to outline some options for future development in the sense of both any unfinished business and any new initiatives that need to be taken.

Probably the first consideration is the importance of viewing this process as *iterative*. To take a key example, the core competences developed are more reflective of the organizational culture of today than tomorrow, although it is possible to develop a fairly clear view of these future requirements, based on the overall framework of competences presented. None the less, one key recommendation is to carry out a job analysis type survey every two years.

A second key point is to develop a better idea of what 'competences' particular *jobs* demand. The core competences approach so far has focused on 'persons specification'. A complementary approach is to identify the key jobs that enable people to develop the skills and abilities required to make an effective transition into managerial roles.

A third point is to ensure that these development and assessment boards are *integrated* with other systems of management development. Using the core competences as a building block in that process would enable better integration between recruitment, selection, appraisal, training and development.

In terms of self-development, the key point is to maximize opportunities for individuals to assess their own training and development plan in conjunction with their management and other career counselling advisers. More work will be needed on this, especially in terms of dispelling any thoughts that lip service is being paid to the developmental aspects.

And that brings us to the last point: continually managing the process so that *all* parties are involved and committed to the vision. That part needs constant care and attention and is perilous to ignore.

Appendix

ACHIEVEMENT ORIENTATION

		1	2	3	4	5
PERSONAL DRIVE	Self-confident and assertive drive to win, with decisiveness and resilience	Decisive even under pressure, assertive and tough-minded in arguing his/her case, very self-confident, shrugs off setbacks	Will commit him/ herself to definite opinions, determined to be heard, can come back strongly if attacked	May reserve judgement where uncertain, but stands firm on important points, aims for compromise, fairly resilient	Avoids taking rapid decisions, takes an impartial coordinator role rather than push own ideas	Doesn't pursue his/ her points, goes along with the group, allows criticism or setbacks to deter him/her
ORGANIZATIONAL DRIVE	Proactive, goal-orientation and sense of urgency, drive to plan and organize to ensure tasks are completed and to high quality	Strong sense of urgency, organizes others to ensure efficient discussion, definite decisions and completion of the task	Aware of digressions and focuses attention on key tasks, plans for the group and keeps track of progress	Talks round the subject but keeps to the point, responds well to attempts to organize the group	Not aware of time, concentrates on discussion, can pull with the group when time is very short	Concerned with immediate arguments not completion of the task, may slow group down by pursuing own interests
IMPACT	Ability to make impact on others through stature and presence, act as role model	Projects strong sense of credibility and natural ability. Likely to make impression in any business situation	Gains and maintains attention and respect. Projects self well	Quite effective in presentation. Can sometimes dominate group. Gains attention and credibility	Does not tend to have stature on issues outside own experience. Treated as peer rather than leader	Lacks natural authority. Contributions overlooked or dismissed by others as less important
COMMUNICATION	Ability to communicate one's own ideas with clarity, structure and brevity	Very clear, structured and concise. Uses concrete examples and paints pictures. Very easy to follow	Gives clear explanations and answers. Knows when own points not clear, and clarifies	Usually clear, occasionally vague or jumps about. Can clarify in response to questions	Rather unstructured, drifts from one idea to another. Sometimes unclear	Vague and unstructured. May miss key points. Others must listen actively and asks questions to clarify

PEOPLE ORIENTATION

	1	2	3	4	5
AWARENESS OF OTHERS	Sensitive to feelings, attitudes, perspectives of others, understand others	Very aware of others, demonstrates sensitivity to their needs. Very client-centred in approach	Aware of others, listens attentively and shows diplomacy. Makes positive efforts to get to understand others	Sometimes gets bound up with own concerns. Can adapt when things go wrong, and listen to others	Overlooks reactions of others when pushing own point. Will occasionally cause friction	Insensitive to others. Focuses on own concerns. Causes friction by unsubtle approach
TEAM MANAGEMENT	Ability to stimulate a productive team climate, where members feel involved and participating. Able to manage interaction of people with different perspectives, conflicting views	Provides process leadership to promote team spirit and enthusiasm. Builds commitment within others to achieve superordinate goals	Encourages others to contribute. Will act as a facilitator for the group. Builds alliances between people and groups.	Balanced approach. Will suggest methods and procedures for how to tackle the task	Tends to overstate the importance and value of one's own contribution. Will reluctantly involve self in group	Prefers individualistic, self-centred approach. Will tend to be in-different to others and will do nothing about it
PERSUA-SIVENESS	Ability to convince others through personal persuasive-ness rather than position power	Very persuasive. Spots others' interests and 'sells to need'. Thinks on feet to counter arguments effectively	Influences effectively most of the time by adapting arguments to others' points of view. Builds on what others say	Tries to influence others but effective-ness will be limited by using same style with everyone	Tries to influence but may use wrong strategy, so will only influence certain people	Expects others to agree, rather than trying to influence them. Will give up when others ignore or resist

JUDGEMENT

	1	2	3	4	5
ANALYTICAL POWER — Ability to grasp new concepts and deal incisively with complex information	Incisive intellect, absorbs complex information rapidly and cuts through to the key points	Able to follow complex arguments and focus on key issues, logical approach	Takes time to come to correct solutions, knows when s/he doesn't know, asks questions to clarify	May oversimplify complex information, or miss a key factor, but able to appreciate where s/he's gone wrong	Not analytical, better with simple data, sometimes misunderstands important issues
STRATEGIC THINKING — Ability to take a long-term perspective, create a vision and take strategic decisions	Challenges assumptions, focuses on broader issues, creates an innovative long-term strategy	Explores several possibilities, questions assumptions, considers longer-term issues	Appreciates and builds on ideas, resourceful, but approach is practical not strategic	Conventional approach, concentrates on immediate task, can accept value of long-term issues	Not interested in ideas, wants quick decisions, focuses on obvious immediate action
COMMERCIAL JUDGEMENT — Shrewd business sense; a hard-headed entrepreneurial approach balancing risks and rewards	Shrewd business judgement, tough-minded and entrepreneurial, strong commercial orientation	Sound awareness of business opportunities, costs & problems, commercial approach	Considers costs/benefits, may lack shrewdness/experience in weighing up business decisions	Relies on estimates and projections, not shrewd in assessing risks, tender-minded approach	Focuses on beliefs not hard facts, assumes issues are straightforward, questionable commercial judgement, rather risk-averse

SITUATIONAL FLEXIBILITY

	1	2	3	4	5
ADAPTIVE ORIENTATION — Ability to read the situation and to adapt so that best possible outcome achieved. Aware of own strengths and weaknesses. Responds effectively to ambiguity and uncertainty	Alert, responsive, client-oriented, sizes up situations rapidly and adapts relevant approach. Quick to learn new approaches	Aware of the situation and the client, usually adopts one style, but can adapt when this not working. Comfortable with ambiguity	Straightforward approach, not quick to spot changes, takes time to recognize problems but will adapt. Will suggest ways of structuring the situation	Uses a single approach under most circumstances, sticks to planned method of approach rather than sizing up clients on the spot. Prefers structure	Single-minded, unresponsive to clients, ploughs ahead regardless, others have to adapt to him/her. Dependent on structured situation

CHAPTER 9

Management succession and organizational change

VALERIE STEWART

Never has it been more difficult or more important than now to produce managers of the future. There is hardly a large organization that has not suffered deep self-analysis or indeed trauma as it has realized that yesterday's success formula is not the same as tomorrow's. In this context, the problem of predicting management potential becomes even more difficult.

Simply put, the difficulty of identifying management potential in today's business climate is three-fold:

- It is always difficult to predict how someone will perform in their next job when records exist only of performance in previous jobs, which may have had different or less severe demands. This is particularly true for certain pivotal jobs which have the strongest impact on the business performance and public perception of the organization, such as first-line management, very senior management and the jobs where a person is Mr or Ms Organization for a particular geographical region.
- In today's rapidly changing business climate, yesterday's success formula is unlikely to hold good for tomorrow. Organizations need to look afresh at what they mean by managerial effectiveness and to plan new ways of identifying and developing this.
- One of the changes in the current business climate is the move towards flatter, shallower organizations. This requires fewer, better managers who will stay longer at any one level

and thus need to exercise more generalist skills. The cost of a wrong promotion is greater because a leaner organization has less room for trial and less opportunity to hide its mistakes.

All these trends mean that succession planning is hampered by the fact that the performance data are not always reliable; the goal-posts have changed; and the consequences of getting it wrong are now more serious.

Organizational growth

All organizations experience clear patterns of growth and transition. Most start small and are characterized by a climate of innovation, high risk-taking, informality, closeness to the market, loose structure, etc. This is the pioneering stage of the organization's growth.

If the product or service is successful and the organization continues to grow, it will inevitably encounter some form of crisis. This is brought about by any or all of the following: the organization has become too big for one manager to manage; it needs more specialist input; it needs finance; the original pioneer has retired or died; the impact of competition (particularly when it learns from the pioneer's mistakes); the informal style has led to 'communication problems'.

Organizations that experience these pioneering problems demonstrate one clear law of human behaviour – in times of crisis people have a tendency to do more of what made them successful *yesterday*. But in the pioneering crisis the last thing the organization needs is more of the 'pioneering' behaviour. What it really requires is systems and controls.

If it survives the crisis, it moves towards a climate in which formal systems are introduced to make things more predictable. Thus, in the systems stage, organizations acquire formal structures; divisions between line and staff; head office and divisions; rules and procedures; formalized planning; specialist functions; and formal relations with unions.

The systems stage also outlives its usefulness. Sooner or later, the systems seem to be running the organization. People grumble about the length of time it takes to get decisions; about a low-risk mentality; too much influence from head office; specialists taking away line managers' discretion; distance from the customer; too much power in the hands of unions; too much bureaucracy; and a tendency to work by the rulebook. If the response to this crisis is the same as during the pioneering crisis – do more of what made the organization successful yesterday – the climate for risk-taking is reduced even further. The rules are tightened; procedures become more onerous; more and more discretion is taken away from line managers; the authority of head office is increased.

The systems crisis can be, and often is, worsened by the fact that managers who are most comfortable with systems and controls are often the least flexible in adopting new styles. Indeed, if you reflect on the growth of industry in the Western world, it is obvious that many of today's big organizations experienced their transition into the systems stage during the late 1960s and early 1970s. These were the times when everyone was busy installing typical systems solutions such as 'management by objectives', formal policies and procedures, performance appraisal systems, computerized succession planning, and so on. These remedies were exactly what they needed at that time. However, one problem is that in doing these things they sent an implicit message to employees that 'what you have to do to be successful is to follow the rules and procedures'.

Twenty years on, these employees are middle managers. The organization may have an over-representation of these managers, who are best at solving problems by applying past experience, unhappy with the risk of going beyond what is prescribed, and less able to envisage new solutions. This is the 'corporate concrete' problem. It is no accident that whenever we work on organization turnaround we find the greatest resistance among middle managers. This is because they are being asked to relinquish the behaviour that was rewarded in the past and that may even have been the reason for their promotion.

A number of organizations are beginning to find a solution to the systems crisis by moving towards the integrated stage. This is characterized by the following climate:

* decentralization
* delegation of authority (as opposed to just work) to line managers
* a move from controlling systems towards enabling systems
* a concerted attempt to 'bust' the bureaucracy
* changes in the role of head office and specialist functions from being 'custodians of the word no' to a combined in-house consultancy and tame merchant bank
* a more entrepreneurial climate, with positive encouragement of risk-taking and innovation
* getting back in touch with the customer
* less emphasis on formal relationships with trade unions and more direct contact between managers and the managed
* a re-emergence of the charismatic leader
* stressing personal leadership at all levels.

One important point is that we do not imply that one stage of growth is necessarily better than another. The important point is one of appropriateness – yesterday's solution is good for yesterday but we must be aware that tomorrow's solution may be different.

What does this say about identifying future managers?

There is a clear difference in the management styles that are appropriate in the different stages of the organization's growth. Some of these differences are shown in Table 9.1. Clearly, when an organization has to manage the transition from one stage to the next, past managerial performance may be an imperfect guide to future success. The values and expectations of the people within the organization may be so different from the future requirements that it is difficult for them to make judgements.

In addition, many organizations are currently moving from the pioneering stage to the systems stage. They wish to make this move as flexible as possible in order to gain the benefits of clarity and formalization, without risking the accompanying ossification characteristic of so many systems organizations in the past. For them, as for the integrated organization, the task is to develop *enabling* systems that act as a frame rather than a cage. Instead of offering people a ceiling that they cannot rise above, enabling systems offer people a floor below which they have no excuse for falling.

These are not the only changes that make it difficult to predict

Table 9.1 Characteristics of organizational growth

Traits	Pioneering	Organizational stage Systems	Integrated
Organization	Flexibility	Hierarchy	Network
Objective	Niche/toe-hold	Market share	Market creation
Focus	Pioneer	Institution	Individual
Style	Informal	Structured	Enabling
Excitement	Novelty	Stabilization	Change
Specialist	Non-existent	Experts	Advisers
Relationships	Informal	Self-sufficient	Networking
Culture	Risk-taking	Precedent	Evolution
Mission	Differentiation	Goals/plans	Identity/values
Leadership	Knowledge	Position	Charisma
Quality	State of the art	Affordable best	No compromise
Expectations	Excitement	Security	Personal growth
Status	Egalitarian	Title/rank	Contribution
Resources	Inventiveness	Cash	Information
Advantage	Novelty	Better sameness	Real difference
Systems	Non-existent	Controlling	Enabling
Customer	Make or break	Locked in	Influential

management potential in changing organizations. Irrespective of the organic state of growth of the organization, factors such as takeovers and mergers, the addition of new products, government edicts, new and perhaps international markets, and competitive activity can all substantially change the requirements for managerial effectiveness.

Identifying management potential

There are two problems to overcome in the identification of management potential. One is the problem of basing predictions about future performance on past behaviour in a different job or range of jobs. This is intrinsically difficult and made worse by the fact that appraisal is often the only consistent record of performance in many organizations. This represents the views of only a handful of managers and also suffers from the fact that many appraisers are not trained to identify potential. It is an appalling thought that performance appraisal forms are typically used to gather data about potential, career aspirations (which may be fed into a computer and used for planning) when in fact many organizations limit their appraisal training to helping managers cope with difficult interviews.

The second problem is more serious and revolves around identifying performance criteria. It is unwise to guess about performance criteria or to choose from a menu, as these usually represent no more than a picture of what is fashionable at the moment, with a sprinkling of the current discontents. There are numerous examples of organizations that have opted for highly sophisticated assessment methods without first identifying the performance criteria best suited to the company's future.

For example, a UK organization with which we worked employed three levels of assessment for first-line managers, middle managers, and senior executives. Never will we forget the discomfort on the face of the appraisal programme manager when someone with the guts to point out the Emperor's new clothes asked him why none of this had stopped the organization from sliding into bankruptcy.

Of course, the company had never been through the process of asking itself whether it was assessing managers on criteria that were relevant to its future. Our experience shows clearly that the performance criteria must be derived from *within* the organization. They must be unique to that organization. They must be owned by the organization and be perceived as part of its development process.

How is this achieved? In our approach, the process starts with highly detailed interviews with managers in, and senior to, the assessed position. The interviewer uses a special technique – the Repertory Grid – which generates precise data and which is totally free from interviewer bias. Thus the performance criteria come from, and are explicitly owned by, line managers in the client organization. These interviews give a highly detailed picture of how the organization's managers define effectiveness at the present time.

The next step is to take that picture to a workshop of senior managers, guiding them if necessary through some of the issues of organization growth and change. The key questions that they consider are: 'Given what we know, or can guess, about the changes that are likely to happen to our organization, what is the survival value of this picture of effectiveness? In what ways does the picture need to change in order to meet the demands of the future?'. This interrogation process leads to a picture of tomorrow's performance criteria. It also highlights the extent of any gaps between today's picture and tomorrow's; if the gap is large, other supporting activities may be necessary to embed the change.

After the interrogation process, the next step is to choose a method or methods for identifying managers for the future. Usually, the best practice is to combine an appropriately designed performance appraisal system with a tailored management assessment programme and psychological testing. Obviously, if the needs of the changing organization are to be best served, the assessment criteria incorporate the results of the diagnosis and interrogation stage. The importance of using line management ownership to gain real commitment to the assessment process becomes obvious here. The developmental information coming from such processes is, in practice, more important than the assessive information. As a result the process is about making people better, as well as judging them.

Conclusion

We describe a process by which the natural changes in organizations can be clearly mapped and discussed with managers; a process for diagnosing without bias or prejudice; a method of identifying and overcoming the gap between present effectiveness and future requirements. The line management ownership of the whole process is crucial and is built into the methodology. The following case studies illustrate some of these points.

A large European railway company

The organization has 25,000 employees. It had been managed with little regard for either financial accountability or quality of service to customers. Largely a passenger railway, it had a base of commuters who felt themselves trapped into using the system but who felt resentful none the less.

The prevailing political atmosphere meant that the government in power was reluctant to take initiatives to improve efficiency. A conservative estimate suggested that the organization could lose 8,000 staff without noticing much difference. It could reduce the workforce to a more appropriate size of 13,000 by investing the savings it made in labour-saving equipment.

Top management suddenly became 'consumer conscious' and anxious to bring about a turnaround in performance. A cynical view would suggest that the impetus for this was a likely change in government, although public discontent was increasingly vocal. Accordingly, top management embarked on a programme of organization turnaround. There was much talk of new organizational missions; 'busting' the bureaucracy; customer awareness; and running the place like a business. However, it was not difficult to detect that many of these actions were cosmetic and that the work necessary to bring about a turnaround was not being done.

A Repertory Grid study of senior and middle managers, undertaken about nine months after the start of the turnaround programme, revealed clearly that managers construed effectiveness under the following three main headings:

- being a good engineer
- looking busy all the time, especially when the boss was around
- seniority.

There was very little mention of the hoped-for factors of business management, financial awareness, customer awareness and interdepartmental teamwork.

We were therefore able to present the top management team with the news that the turnaround programme had not yet reached the point where its values were part of the routine thinking of senior and middle managers. We were able to convince them that much more energy and commitment needed to be put in before the programme would achieve results.

A multinational oil company

This company commissioned a Repertory Grid study among its middle managers. Some 200 managers were interviewed (making this one of the largest grid studies ever conducted) to determine today's criteria of effective management. The main performance descriptions, or 'constructs', are summarized in Table 9.2.

The question was asked: 'What is the survival value of this picture of effectiveness?' In particular, we drew attention to the large amount of 'managing upwards'; the comparatively small emphasis on lateral relations, teamwork, or customer awareness; the highly cerebral nature of the constructs; the lack of emphasis on personal and staff development; the lack of emphasis on personal qualities such as leadership. It became apparent that this company was heading for, if not actually in, the systems crisis. A distinctively new management style would be needed in the future.

A *large multinational manufacturing company*

This company wanted to assess the capabilities of its young managers to run operations in Africa. In the past, this responsibility was given to graduate trainees after they had spent a few years working in head office. However, not all the assignments had been

Table 9.2   Criteria of effective management

Performance descriptions	Response (%)
• Relations with head office – managing the system and paperwork, knowing the right people and procedures	30
• Communication with own subordinates – clear delegation, instructions and feedback	15
• Analytical ability to comprehend large amount of information, diagnose problems, numerical skills	15
• Planning – ability to formulate clear, rational plans over a five-year horizon at least	10
• Decision-making – ability and willingness to take decisions within own level of authority	10
• Presentation skills – cogent written or verbal presentation of an argument or situation	10
• Stress management – ability to handle large volumes of work and cope with conflicting demands	5
• Political awareness – understanding of national and international politics, pressures and influences	5

successful. Given the high cost of failure, the company wanted to be more clear about what it should look for in a suitable candidate.

A Repertory Grid study was conducted with a sample of managers from the UK head office and Africa itself. This revealed clear differences in the qualities thought to be effective in the two areas. Head office managers concentrated heavily on the following qualities: planning and analysis skills; rational decision-making; careful preparation of cases, including written communication skills. By contrast, the Africa-based managers concentrated on stamina and stress management; the ability to think on one's feet and cope without a formal support system; informal, largely verbal, communications skills; leadership ability and industrial relations skills.

The result was an assessment programme that revealed that a number of people regarded as non-conformists in head office would – and did – do well in Africa. A training and development programme was designed to bring about a more multi-skilled approach in both streams of managers and a smoother interchange between the two locations.

A governmental welfare department

The department asked for a Repertory Grid study to determine how employees perceived effective management. This exercise was part of a large organizational change programme which involved decentralizing decision-making. For the first time, local managers were being given responsibility for financial management. Another initiative was a programme that aimed to incorporate the various values and customs of ethnic minorities into the department. The whole effort took place at a time of rapid changes in government policy on social welfare.

The grid study had some interesting outcomes. One piece of good news was the extent to which multicultural values and activities had become part of the middle managers' thinking. More worrying was the fact that the bulk of the constructs concentrated on personal qualities such as integrity and commitment to the department's values. This was no bad thing in itself, but there was hardly any mention of the type of plain management skills that were needed in the new climate. Another concern was that these managers had very few constructs to do with policy matters – either communicating upwards to influence policy decisions or communicating downwards to help their staff in dealings with the public.

A further divergence in values was revealed when we analysed the difference in constructs between the career civil servants, whose job patterns typically involved moving from one government department to another, and the committed social welfare managers. The former group clearly saw their task as implementing government policy first, with client need very much a secondary consideration. The second group saw their job as doing all they could for the client in the teeth of government policy. This division had implications for the selection of people to fill very senior management jobs.

The study, and the succeeding interrogation phase, gave rise to a targeted training and development plan. This placed special emphasis on the development of business management skills; a performance appraisal system and management assessment system based on new performance criteria; and serious consideration of career planning and management issues. It was also used to give a strong strategic steer to the general organization change programmes, because we now knew the basic values from which we were starting.

A *major health insurance company*

This company asked for assistance in determining a better profile against which to select and train salesmen who were responsible for selling private health care to businesses as an employee benefit. The call-to-order ratio among the existing sales force was unsatisfactory and getting worse.

A grid study of sales staff, combined with field observation of sales calls, revealed the following two problems:

- Many salesmen viewed personnel directors as their client, not realizing that the decision to offer private health insurance is a board decision. Their main task, therefore, was to make bullets for the personnel director to fire at the board.
- Salesmen clearly saw their job as selling the *idea* of private health insurance to companies – instead of selling their own services.

120

Typically, they would arouse the personnel director's interest in private health insurance to the point where she/he would call for competitive quotations.

We were therefore able to make some simple and effective recommendations for training salespeople, which led to a significant improvement in sales performance.

CHAPTER 10

Towards organizational teamworking

WENDY BRINER & FRANK TYRRELL

In 1984, a group of people working for Ashridge Teamworking Services (ATS) produced a model for outstanding team performance. The model was the result of action research. It consolidated consulting practice and identified the characteristics, strategies and behaviours of teams that clearly performed better than average. The model consists of several core elements, with clusters of specific activities in each element, which lead to improved performance. This is illustrated in Figure 10.1.

The ATS model assumes that teams are determined by the task – they are not just the team that appears on the organization chart. In addition to the leader and easily identifiable team members, teams will also incorporate invisible, part-time members who may be within the organization or who may be clients or suppliers. Additionally, every permanent or temporary team has a sponsor, who has an interest in the results of their activities but who is not responsible for day-to-day execution. The sponsor is usually a more senior manager. This view of organizational teamworking broadens the concept of teambuilding and sets it realistically in the organizational context. So it can be called organizational teamworking.

Leadership and membership

The ATS model considers both leadership and membership as key elements to successful teamworking. In terms of leadership, for

THE VISION IS

SUPERTEAM

the strategies and the skills are

Negotiating Success Criteria

The Team Apart

Managing the Outside

The Team Together

Planning the What

Membership

Planning the How

Leading the Team

Source: Hastings, Bixby and Chaundry-Lawton (1986)

Figure 10.1 The Ashridge teamworking approach

example, setting the standards and creating an environment for success for the team are clearly a vital activity. ATS consulting work indicated that helping the leader to understand how he/she did this was, unsurprisingly, essential to success. But more importantly, it became apparent that creating an environment for success can be accomplished in many different ways. This is largely dictated by the individual leader's preferences and particular strengths and weaknesses.

When trying to make specific teams more effective, it became clear that all leaders must be willing to alter at least a small but significant part of what they do and how they do it. In some instances, the leader may be required to change to a greater extent than team members. However, the adaptation that the leader makes matches the modifications of members' competences. If they get out of synchronization, any improvement in performance or personal engagement will be lost and may lead to cynicism among the team.

Membership as a concept is far less well articulated than leadership. Many people see membership as something that *happens* to them and leaves them relatively powerless. Membership can be viewed as an active state, unlike 'followership' which has a passive sheeplike quality. ATS consulting work often focuses on helping members to test the boundaries of their own assumptions and perception of norms of behaviour. This enables them to be demanding, influential and enabling members, who can play a significant part in improving team performance. This benefits both the individual members and the corporate organization.

Our definition of membership is that it is the tension between the individual's personal orientation to life and the organization's assumptions about the attitudes, needs, feelings and concerns of members. This leads to sets of values, norms, processes and behaviours that condition how members and organizations deal with each other. If there is very high dissonance between the two, the individual members may leave and go somewhere more compatible. Usually, there are sufficient areas of overlap between the two sets of assumptions to make a workable compromise. There may be areas of tension also, where disagreement causes friction and demotivation.

The personal orientation of employees is clearly complex and may vary during their working life. If they are personally engaged in the organization's purpose and values, there will be a high degree of overlap concerning what they want to do, how they contribute to the organization and how the organization treats them.

These views of leadership and membership and the balances between them seem to influence the effectiveness of teams. Through the experience of working with a wide variety of businesses that were seeking to adapt or change significantly, it has been observed that the nature of the organizational environment impinges on both what leaders and members can do and *how* they can do it. This leads to the consideration of what problems have been encountered and what implications this has for improving team performance.

Issues arising from teamwork

Creating teamworking cultures

Many organizations aim to be better at teamworking, not least because the current management literature suggests that flexible, low-hierarchy organizations can respond rapidly to external pressures. This seems to be particularly true for high-tech companies and new organizations which have set themselves up with these values and traditions and then work hard to achieve them.

The push towards teamworking is more difficult for bureaucratic companies with high volumes of standard products or services, delivered through relatively stable channels. A wholesale adoption of a teamworking culture may be inappropriate or even unfeasible. The following ideas may be more appropriate:

- Better collaborative working within the normal channels of work organization and communications, to make the wheels turn more smoothly and rapidly.
- Temporary structures such as taskforces, working parties or corrective action teams which can act as vehicles for changing certain aspects of the organization's activities. Temporary teams are also very useful for handling uncertainty and integrating diverse, cross-functional interests. Not all temporary teams succeed, however, as they sometimes need to cut across organizational norms in order to be effective. If they go too far, they may be squashed or misunderstood. If they stay within accepted practices, they may not go fast enough or be radical enough. If they are to succeed, it is critical that teams get the right combination of strategies and behaviour.

These observations raise questions concerning the different interpretations of what teamworking is and the kind of collaborative practices that are likely to succeed in organizations with little experience of teamworking.

Crossing the Rubicon

Moving from more formal interactions to more collaborative ways of working is not always easy. Leaders and members sometimes put themselves at risk and frequently progress much more slowly than expected, even in organizations with conducive conditions.

As Greenwood and Hinings (1988) point out, there is little collected information about unsuccessful attempts to change organizations, small groups or individuals. However, changing is a more complex and difficult activity than is usually admitted.

The following common difficulties are encountered when trying to improve performance:

- Individual leaders or members who step too far out of line, or who seem to be 'too good', may suffer a backlash. They may be actively undermined or castigated for arrogance.
- Attempts to test the boundaries of leaders or members, by encouraging them to challenge their normal ways of doing things through asking questions or involving other people, may run aground because they seem too risky. Individuals may feel that their beliefs about the leader and the organization are being too deeply challenged. The implications of the new rules of the game may seem impossible or unfair. So the new competences may not be tested out or they may be so tentatively tried that they are doomed to failure.
- Organizations that openly proclaim their vision for change find that there is a huge web of complex and interrelated systems, attitudes, values, meanings and ways of working that inhibit movement. The mass of 'interpretive schemes and processes' (Greenwood and Hinings 1988) that exist in organizational life reduce the impact of, or even abort, initiatives for change. If leaders and members have to cross many organizational interpretive systems, improving performance will tend to be a slow process. Therefore improvements in teamworking are likely to be most effective when they enhance elements that already exist in the organization.

Leadership styles

A brief survey of organizations that are performing reasonably well or even very well indicates that there is a wide range of leadership styles that are conducive to high performance. It is not just the open, participative, visioning leader who is able to mobilize high performance effectively. Other leadership and membership styles can, and do, produce very high performance.

Team performance can be improved by investigating how the leader and members work together within their organizational environment to ensure that it is in optimal balance. No style of leadership or membership is in itself better or worse than another. A style can be appropriate or not, and competences applied or not.

A model of leadershp and membership performance

Taking into consideration the questions that arise about teamworking plus an understanding of what produces high performance (identified in the ATS model), it is possible to formulate a hypothesis about how to apply these principles to a wide variety of organizations.

The hypothesis is that the links between leadership and membership competences in high performing businesses are conditioned by the organizational environment. Different organizational environments can be very effective if the elements of leadership and membership are congruent. If improved performance is to be sustained, shifts in leaders' or members' competences must be in tune with how the organization is evolving. The ATS model and its seven elements is a helpful diagnostic tool to determine what has the most impact on performance. It is possible to isolate strategies and competences that are coherent with the *dominant coalition* of any particular organization. The dominant coalition is the result of the leadership and membership style which produces formal and informal ways of interacting that characterize an organization.

ATS' leadership and membership performance model (see Figure 10.2) assumes that the changes in performance are primarily within the *organizational environment*. The idea of an environment refers to the basic nature of the organization in terms of how power is used, how it is structured and how the culture is described. An expansion or exploration of new behaviours or values may be used to enhance or extend the existing archetype. Evolutionary shifts may be accomplished if new approaches and expertise are found to be useful and therefore easily incorporated. Anthropologists talk of a similar idea in 'cultural drift' where, through exposure to or casual contact with new ideas, customs and behaviours migrate from one culture to another. This tends to occur because of the perceived effectiveness of the new customs and is certainly not an imposed process.

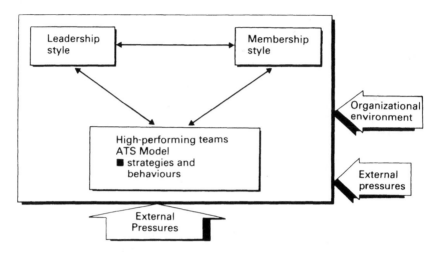

Figure 10.2 Leadership and membership performance model

There is currently much discussion about the need for organizations to shift fundamentally from one organizational environment to another. This model offers some insights into how multi-layered and complex this activity tends to be. While appreciating the issues involved in a major shift, we are focusing on strategies for improving performance which do not require radical upheaval. *Mutation* rather than revolution is the approach being investigated.

Many organizations are trying to modify their organizational environment at varying speeds and intensities. Balancing the leadership style with the membership style can result in significant increases in performance that build on or extend a major part of the original archetype.

Leadership and membership styles in different environments

Building on Charles Handy's (1976) and Roger Harrison's (1972) definitions of organizational cultures, five environments have been identified as useful classifications. These are teamworking, expert, networking, power and bureaucratic organizations.

Miller and Frieson (1988) have suggested that organizations are 'configurations composed of tightly interdependent and mutually supportive elements such that the importance of each element can best be understood by making reference to the whole configuration'. The organizational environment is composed of a number of themes. These are not exhaustive but illustrate how a configuration is composed and therefore what conditions the way in which organizations operate. Although not all of the elements will be equally important in a specific configuration, all of them will be entwined in the fabric of the organizational environment.

Configuration themes include:

- the structure or nature of industry and therefore the tasks to be performed;
- the history of the founders and the major stages of crisis in the organization's life;
- the pressure of various external demands;
- the cultural influences, the 'way things happen';
- the prevailing values and business direction;
- the use of controls and rewards, formal and informal.

There is no assumption that any one organizational environment is inherently more effective than any other. All can, and do, work outstandingly well or very badly. Teamworking organizations and the organizations of experts seem to be on the increase. Although networking organizations *can* be found, they are far from common. Currently power and bureaucratic organizations seem to be the most common in Europe. Clearly, few organizations are pure environments and many may be a combination of several characteristics. The archetypes are meant to be guidelines that help to elucidate the links between leadership, membership and organizational environments, so that strategies for improved performance can be developed.

The main features of the five organizational environments, and their leadership and membership styles, will now be outlined.

Power organizations

The organizational environment has the following characteristics:

* clear direction, set priorities and performance standards, clear controls (if these criteria are not met, it's 'Good bye!')

* rewards and punishments are set by the top person
* hierarchical (know your place and stay in it)
* teams and individuals are divided, survival of the fittest
* delegation to and reliance on loyal individuals, groups of courtiers cluster around the top people
* information and communication are the tools of power and are not shared
* resources are given to those who perform and play the game
* personal energy is rewarded if you stay on the tracks
* products or services are often narrowly defined and mature in the product lifecycle.

Examples include Hanson, Ford and GEC.

The leadership style in power organizations has the following characteristics:

* vision and direction come from the top (this is either imposed or sold because it is attractive, but it is generally non-negotiable)
* charismatic, so encouraging 'the cult of the boss' through many stories about the leader's achievement and his or her high personal energy
* rules are made and changed as seen fit, resulting in sharp and rapid action
* information is retained, secrecy is often high
* a high profile is taken, letting his/her will be done, both internally and externally
* depends on individuals and deals with individuals instead of groups.

The membership style of the organization has the following characteristics. Members:

* know what the score is and try to make it come right; if it is wrong, times will be hard
* blame anyone or anything if something doesn't work out
* are adversarial, undermining, plotting and indulge in power games
* have scope to act, as long as they succeed
* do not declare anything unless it is successful

* do not risk too much, in case they are wrong
* stay in their respective areas, do not try to help others.

Bureaucracy organizations

The organizational environment has the following characteristics:

* committees create direction based on careful and methodical analysis; dependence on data; papers and learned approaches are valued; use of precedent
* implementation of plans is achieved through processes, procedures and methods; linear and mechanical; formal systems exist for pay and reward, promotion and career management, budgeting and control, appeals for wrong doing
* clear job responsibilities, duties, communication and decision-making patterns; formal boundaries are made clear by symbols; emphasis is placed on the hierarchy
* slow response to changes that cannot be legislated for; high investment in the status quo
* respect for expertise and boundaries
* resources are given to those who work the system
* production processes are geared to standard outputs.

Examples include BP, British Telecom, Shell, DHSS and McDonalds.
   The leadership style in bureaucratic organizations has the following characteristics:

* the leader is one of the system; there are few myths about this individual, who tends to be one who confers and who knows how to operate through the established rules
* leaders rarely have a strong personalized vision and will promote the agreed direction down the appropriate channels
* power is vested in the position and power of budgetary control
* decisions are made through consensus and formal procedures; there is a greater emphasis on debating issues than on action
* leaders deal with people through formal groupings, e.g. standing committees

The photofit manager

The membership style of a bureaucractic organization has the following features. Members:

* who work the system well are respected and given scope
* who rock the boat are mistrusted; individuals who shine can have a hard time
* find it hard to break outside their own boundaries as this will be seen as a threat to the proper functioning of the whole body; they are not encouraged to go directly to people
* do things the right way, rather than do the right thing
* know the rules and use them skilfully.

Teamworking organizations

The organizational environment has the following characteristics:

* frequently changing organizational structures
* changing constellations of people who get together formally and informally to accomplish tasks or solve problems
* vision and overall direction is widely understood and constantly reinforced; values are often explicit
* tight procedures for budgeting and headcount; a lot of space to implement as managers wish
* *few hierarchical boundaries between people*; pay and rewards go to high achievers; everyone is motivated by success; people are highly valued and well treated; occasionally impatient with long-term activities
* work is often responsive and with many variations.

Examples include Hewlett Packard, Rapid Recall, Digital and Child Care Unit.

The leadership style in teamworking organizations has the following characteristics. Leaders:

* are custodians of the corporate vision or mission and constantly make it relevant to current issues
* actively propagate the values of how things should be done
* are very accessible and move around formally and informally in the organization; they listen and respond even-handedly

* create an environment that energizes people to contribute to the best of their ability
* are seen to be close to the activity; many stories and legends exist that illustrate the leader's acclaimed behaviour
* look after the image of the company outside as well as inside.

The membership style of the organization has the following characteristics. Members:

* get on with their jobs as best they can because activity is rewarded; success and achievement are also rewarded
* cross boundaries to find out who knows or can help
* expect to be taken into account and to be heard; their individual worth is based on their contribution, not their status; the person closest to the action knows everything that is happening
* have high energy and personal commitment
* expect the organization to take care of people and to be fair.

Expert organizations

An increasing number of organizations exist to provide professional/expert technical services. These organizations are either independent or coexist within other organizations, but at a distinct arm's length. They consist of professionally qualified experts doing knowledge-based work that requires a detailed educational background.

The organizational environment has the following characteristics:

* the professional or educational basis provides the often unquestionable right and authority to make decisions
* clients give instructions or provide briefs and get the correct answer (this means they often need to ask the 'right' questions)
* one professional cannot comment or criticize another's work; some professions are perceived as superior
* strong hierarchy
* managing the enterprise is seen as unnecessary, distasteful or not proper work (it should just happen).

The photofit manager

Examples include architects, research scientists, legal departments, consultants, NHS general practitioners, solicitors, accountants.

The leadership style in expert organizations has the following characteristics:

* the most senior professional, as judged by the professional criteria for success, takes the role of leader
* leaders value and spend time on professional work
* formal systems take care of the organization of work and financial processes
* leaders are conscious of their image compared with other professionals
* senior people deal with important clients.

The membership style of the organization has the following characteristics. Members:

* adhere to a strict hierarchy of professionals; juniors are treated differently; non-professionals do not exist
* have to win their spurs and overcome professional hurdles
* keep to what they have been asked to do; do not ask questions
* keep separate from others.

Networking organizations

The organizational environment has the following characteristics:

* members actively and thoughtfully subscribe to what is done and how it is done
* strong self-determination to opt in or out
* strong shared values, which act as organizational glue
* simple but strict administrative central control, which holds the 'spider's web' organizational structure together.

Examples include the FI Group, Association of Management Education and Training, Xerox, ATS.

The leadership style in networking organizations has the following characteristics:

* leadership rotates easily according to the activity, competence and interest of individuals
* leadership tasks, such as managing and promoting the corporate image, are shared, both inside the organization and outside
* leaders create an environment that achieves the task and matches the variable needs of the members
* leaders maintain sufficient stability at the core in order to keep the organization viable.

The membership style of the organization has the following characteristics:

* members are there because they want to be; they accept the terms or work to change them
* members are often self-selecting but have a 'working in' period to earn credits
* everyone is an owner; all fight for resources and recognition as needed
* all should make proposals to maintain and improve the organization as they have a strong sense of responsibility for its destiny.

High performance in the five organizational environments

The ATS model can be applied to augment performance but as the performance model suggests, this will be achieved through appropriate strategies and behaviours.

Negotiating success criteria has been found to be a critical part of high performance. It is worth considering as an illustration how this might be approached in each organizational environment.

Power

In power organizations, the overt success criteria tend to be hard and are often to do with financial measures. Standards are imposed, and are met, but not generally exceeded. Soft criteria are important,

135

though often difficult to determine. They may well be taken as read. However, the leader expresses the hard criteria in very clear terms. Teams will normally be operating within tight boundaries. Members may be unwilling to cooperate with each other in public, but may be able to make small coalitions of mutual interest.

Performance improvements can be achieved by checking individual motivation when assembling the team (it may be better to exclude an unwilling member). Teams should ensure that the members are quite clear that membership will have some positive value to them. Other steps include the following:

- External success criteria should be gauged from every source possible. There may be many stakeholders who need to be considered. This means using a wide range of contacts from all the members. Issues may be raised informally in 'what if' form initially, so as not to raise unachievable expectations with an important stakeholder and so create ripples.
- By gaining extra information from the client or customer about the purpose and use of the output, the team is more likely to be right first time. Disruption free delivery is very important in a power environment.
- The activities of a team will often be regarded as suspicious or competitive. It is important to clarify the political implications of the team's activities, both for the team itself and for some of the organization stakeholders.

Bureaucracy

In bureaucracies, teams tend to be forced to adhere to centrally imposed success criteria. Hard criteria tend to be dominated by central budget assumptions. Expectations are often low: a percentage increase on last year's sales or profit is typically demanded, which does not require dramatic changes. Soft criteria are normally conditioned by strong organizational norms to do with communication patterns, media and form. External relationships, standards of conduct and image are also significant. Great emphasis is placed on doing things the right way to earn credits.

Effective teams in this environment can do the following to improve the negotiation and clarification of success criteria:

- Gain clarity about real expectations and constraints by addressing within the team any concerns about suboptimal performance and any items of negative feedback from outside and inside the organization. By distilling these, the team leader has a thought-out set of issues which can be raised with the bosses or other influential people. Further clarity and commitment can be gained by contacting suppliers and customers to agree guidelines and to establish good-quality feedback systems.
- Often more assertive behaviour by the team leader and members will ensure that all issues are raised so that a clear, not fudged, response is gained.
- Anticipated conflicts of priority can also be raised and discussed at an early stage so that senior managers are prepared and confident.
- Once agreed, success criteria should be written down and distributed so that no mistake can be made about original intentions. To meet urgent needs, teams that are performing well in changing conditions may need to be brave enough to renegotiate some components of success at times other than the annual or fixed stages.
- Conflicts of criteria should be dealt with by escalating them to the appropriate level in the organization. Support this by a sound written case. Conflicts can sometimes be resolved by informal 'off the record' moves by an appropriate team member.

Teamworking

Teamworking organizations often have complex internal structures with visible client and supplier/contractor interfaces. They negotiate success criteria in a comprehensive way and continue to address issues as they arise. For this reason many people in a team will be involved in the clarification and negotiation of success criteria. Some useful steps in this process include the following:

- At each stage in the development of a new piece of work, plot the full range of internal and external stakeholders. Use all team members to discuss emergent success criteria, both soft and hard. Map these and raise specific examples of how they are significant. Test them with the team and the other stakeholders, ideally at the same time. Circulate the full outcome of initial negotiations to all parties, so that gaps and conflicts are clear to all. This may well mean involving parties earlier than technical needs would normally demand. End users or sub-contractors could be drawn in, in order to ensure clarity and comprehensiveness in all agreements.

- A mechanism must be available for handling changes in success criteria. In many cases, what is wanted only clearly emerges as work proceeds. In other cases, the environment changes in a way that forces significant changes of direction. Changes have to be discussed and all parties persuaded of the need for them. Motivation can be badly affected if this is not done in a way that creates understanding.

Expert

In professional cultures, discussion and negotiation of success criteria can be touchy. The assumption is often made that professionals will do the right thing because they are professional. Discussion is somehow an intrusion or an insult to their competence. Differences in success criteria can seem to go to the root of the professional's self-respect. They tend to be resolved by *fait accompli* or seniority. Once the customer's or internal stakeholders' wants are taken into consideration, enormous gulfs can open up, with major dissatisfaction all round. For professional teams to work well the following suggestions apply:

- Arrange for a regular, visible feedback mechanism from customers, suppliers, internal stakeholders, secretaries, clerical staff and bosses. Analyse the feedback and take this into account in action plans. Success criteria that indicate quality, such as administrative back-up or interpersonal considerations, may often seem trivial to professionals yet these may be the only tangible ways for customers to judge the service.
- Take time to ensure all members are on board with agreed success criteria. Listen to team members' concerns, suggestions or disagreements but keep discussing the criteria until authentic agreement is reached. Include user groups and members of

administrative staff in discussions to ensure outside voices are heard.

Network

Teams in network organizations will often have grown around a common interest or purpose. The success criteria agreed for any activity may need to accommodate some individual demands given the basis of buying into the team. Good teams often tolerate a level of ambiguity.

End user or client success can often be used as a major element in producing common agreement. A danger is that soft criteria, especially relating to how the team works, may be dominant and can raise tensions that detract from task performance. The following factors should be considered:

- In order to succeed network teams may need a good deal of continuing discussion to clarify success criteria. This needs to be carefully managed. Agreements should be tested by using specific examples of what might be done. Team leaders may need to demonstrate considerable patience and 'chairmanship' skill.
- Task outputs and schedules may be written, circulated and used as monitoring devices for progress. Members of user groups can be useful for clarifying user requirements.

Conclusion

Leadership and membership styles and the organizational environment influence the particular strategies and competences that a team may need to use to improve its performance. This assumes that, while the team is largely conforming to the basic organizational environment, it may also be trying to modify some interpretive schemes. The ATS model focuses on the areas where attention on this process will improve performance. However, the approach that can be employed needs to be varied to be in tune with the elements.

References

Greenwood, R. and Hinings, C. (1988), 'Organizational design, types, tracks and the dynamics of strategic change', *Organization Studies*.

Handy, C. (1976), 'So you want to change your own organization. Then first identify its culture', *Management Education and Development* vol. 7.

Harrison, R. (1972), 'Understanding your organization's character', *Harvard Business Review*, May–June.

Hastings, C., Bixby, P. and Chaudry-Lawton, R. (1986) *Superteams: A Blueprint for Organizational Success* (London: Fontana).

Miller and Frieson (1988), in Greenwood and Hinings, op. cit.

CHAPTER 11

Action profiling at Kodak

MIKE O'FARRELL

In November 1986, I looked at my department. It was full of experienced, energetic, professional people who were working flat out producing some terrific results. But in analysing the situation, I could see that our goals were sometimes uncoordinated and that people were not working together as well as they could. People's talents were being wasted. Tasks that could take one manager a few days to carry out were taking several weeks to be completed by other managers, whose strengths lay in different areas. Communication was superficially strong but at management meetings people were apprehensive about opening up to discuss problems. From a personal angle I felt that my management team were not approaching me as freely as they should to discuss the ins and outs of current projects.

In short, the department was working, but I knew it could work better. The problem was that I could not put my finger on the button that would make it happen. I know that identifying a problem is the major hurdle to solving it. In this case, however, identifying the problem was just the beginning.

I knew that at a corporate level Kodak worked with the consultancy McKinsey and Co for strategic organization and decisions, but I felt this was too high level for what I needed. I have also been involved with tick box analyses/methods which provide a snapshot view of performance. However, I also dismissed this approach because it does not provide a tailored assessment of a group or indicate how to progress once you have assimilated the information.

Action profiling

My first course of action was, therefore, to talk to the head of human resources. I told her that I wanted a specialist who could take my management team, break it into bits and then put it back together so that we were all going down the same path. Did she know an organization that could do that? I prepared myself to tell her that I did not want the usual approaches when she took the wind out of my sails by telling me she knew just the company I needed to talk to, Professional People Development (PPD).

Anita Hall of PPD visited me and discussed action profiling.[1] She explained that this would involve taking each member of the management team and interviewing him or her for between one and two hours. These interviews would be videoed. Anita would then analyse her notes from the meetings together with the video tape and produce a decision-making profile for each person and a personal action plan. At this stage we could all meet and discuss how we could move forward as a management team.

Personally, I was a bit sceptical. I decided to test the water before committing the complete management team. I asked Anita to profile one of my managers, John, who I felt I knew fairly well.

The results were very good. Anita first reviewed the profile with John. I then joined them both so that she could review the main points with me. Both John and I agreed that Anita had identified his strengths and weaknesses correctly. More importantly, she had been able to explain how John's decision-making process worked and why he was more successful on certain projects than others. I was convinced of the value of action profiling and asked PPD to carry out profiles on the whole management team.

So how exactly does PPD work? First, it breaks down the decision process into the following three major areas:

- *Attending*: the attending stage is when we stand back and review the facts of the problem and how it could be tackled.
- *Intending*: the intention stage is concerned with reviewing the various methods of tackling a problem and deciding on the most appropriate route.
- *Committing*: the commitment stage is about how we carry out timely, future-oriented actions.

This is obviously a simplistic view as these decision processes get combined and can fall in any order, depending on the strengths of the individual.

Each of these stages is then subdivided. In the attending stage, different ways of approaching the problem and the fact-finding investigation that goes with it are explored. The intention stage is broken down into evaluating the methods available and deciding on the preferred route of action. The final commitment stage divides into the timing associated with putting the plan into action, the anticipation of possible outcomes and the development of contingency plans for each potential outcome.

When this was explained to me it made sense that any action could be split into these segments. The key to how we carry these out and why we should be aware of this lies in our personal motivation, which is unique to each of us.

Involvement

At each of these major phases – giving attention to a problem, formulating an intention and making a commitment – there is another facet that makes the whole process even more alive and practical. Anita Hall explains it: 'At each of these major stages we relate to each other in the team through our involvement or lack of it. Therefore, knowing whether or not you comfortably share your thought processes with others allows us to identify possible problem areas and to define a course of action.'

As an example of this process, my own profile revealed that I was very independent in my thought process when I was assessing a problem. I liked to think through the options and sort them out in my own mind first before I talked to the team. Externally, people would think I had gone blank, that I was ignoring the problem or that I did not know how to tackle it. If I had been able to share my thoughts more or if my team had asked me about the options I was reviewing, we could have worked more closely together. However, when my managers asked me to talk in the past, I was rarely forthcoming. Because they could not understand my reticence, they were often deterred from making another approach.

143

Having defined each individual's decision-making process and inclination towards sharing or private interaction, the next step is to assess their ability to adapt to situations and to identify with other people's points of view. Both of these points are crucial in a team. People who cannot easily adapt to a new situation must be allowed a longer period of adjustment. Again, if someone has a problem identifying with another team member's viewpoint it is important to consider how this person can feel a greater sense of involvement with the viewpoint or concept. Do you take greater time to explain the background to the situation? Do you share the process of how you reached that conclusion and what the important issues are? Do you talk about the importance of timing to 'the business' and where the concept can take us on a step-by-step basis? Once we understand where each of us concentrates our energies, we find whole new ways of relating and communicating.

As part of the process, the technique also identifies someone's capacity to handle multiple projects and whether working in this way hinders their thought process. It also identifies exactly how people approach problems – do they make a decision and commit themselves to a course of action before evaluating all the options, or do they follow the logical route of attending, intending and then committing?

This aspect has proved to be a major influence on how I currently group people together to tackle projects. If I know that two people on a project are not good at researching information, it is important to give them the back-up of a person strong in this area. Equally, I can ensure that a major project with few external influences and relationships is handled by a strong, single-project-minded team leader.

Benefits to Kodak

So what exactly are the benefits of PPD's decision-making profiles?

The major benefit is that each individual in the team understands where he or she needs help in order to ensure that each problem is completely addressed from every angle. This is where the real change has come about in Kodak. In order to reap this benefit, I assess projects before I hand them out. This ensures that I do not set unrealistic targets for people who have inappropriate decision-making processes to tackle the problem.

Secondly, I group people together on the basis of their decision-making processes to ensure that, where possible, there is a well-balanced team. The most noticeable effect of these changes is in the way people are now working together. My managers no longer hesitate to ask me how we are going to address a situation. They know now that I can be a very private person, so they have to push me to open up my thought process. Conversely, I know that they need to understand what is going on, so I make more effort to be receptive to their questions.

Each individual in our team now understands how the others work. They have no problem in saying, 'You had better let me handle this as it is easier for me to investigate and explore situations' or 'I need your help in this as you are the smart one at anticipating results – what do you think will happen if . . . .?' It is fascinating to see people open up and interact so closely, recognizing their individual strengths, and not being ashamed to admit their weaknesses in particular areas. Everybody works at developing the areas where they are weaker in order to create a stronger team.

The initial analyses took about six months to complete for the whole team. We then worked closely with PPD to apply development techniques for individuals and the team as a whole. This involved other parts of the group over a 10–12-month period. Throughout all of this, individuals at PPD became part of our team. After the initial analysis, we found that they worked with us to put their recommendations in place. However, they gradually became involved in our day-to-day operations. We found them contributing to our projects and even at times participating in the decision-making process and questioning us to ensure that we had considered all the options. This 100 per cent involvement throughout the project enabled us to accept and better understand the decision-making profile assessments and to fully utilize the knowledge gained in everyday working situations.

By focusing the correct resources on a project we now complete work more successfully and in a shorter timescale. This obviously has had a significant effect on profitability and particularly on quality. The morale of the team has been boosted tremendously because each individual now feels a greater sense of involvement through concentrating on the areas where his or her strengths lie. When difficult projects run into problems, the morale stays high because we can talk about the best way to tackle the situation. Again, everybody feels involved.

Since carrying out this decision-making project I have been promoted to my current position as consumer products division manager within Kodak. I believe that action profiling was a major contributor to the success of the previous team and that it will be a significant help in my new division. The results I have seen convince me that the understanding between managers gained from their decision-making profile produces a quantum leap in productivity, profitability and individual growth.

Note

1 The Action Profile System is a registered trademark of Action Profilers International.

CHAPTER 12

From vision to action

ERIC MITCHELL

Much of the current debate about effective management performance has concentrated on knowledge, skills and values. Internal drive is, however, another important dimension of the competent manager.

To be both skilful and effective, managers require data, information, maps, images and conceptual frameworks (i.e. knowledge) to carry out the thinking, logical part of their work. They also need to take into account their own feelings and the feelings, orientations and aspirations of the people with whom they are interdependent. However, neither of these factors is sufficient; managers need to have the will, motivation, drive or energy to put their thoughts and abilities into action.

This chapter is a description of work that has been done in this area. It describes the need for change in the way some organizations are operating as well as the theory behind a management development programme that has been formulated by QUARTO, a group of management consultants and trainers.

Tidying up management education

One glance at world economic patterns reveals that there is no obvious link between economic success and management education. Japan particularly illustrates this. The obvious dominance of Japanese companies is worrying when the educational approach is so different compared with the USA and the UK. Handy (1987) asks why Britain produces only 1,200 MBA graduates a year while the USA produces 70,000, West Germany and France none and Japan only 60? But are we right to follow the US pattern, or is this an attempt to 'tidy up' the education of managers to make it more organized, respectable and professional?

Aldous Huxley said: 'The wish to impose order upon confusion, to bring harmony out of dissonance and unity out of multiplicity, is a kind of intellectual instinct, a primary and fundamental urge of the mind' (Lorenz, 1988). The wish to impose order is understandable but it has dangers. Using education in this way can condition and stifle imagination, stop initiative and experimentation. The growth of institutions has almost always followed the same lines and usually results in rules and bureaucracy stifling individuality.

The *IPM Digest* in Britain reported in July 1988:

> Dr John Constable . . . has questioned proposals to create a Chartered Management Institute which would confer a set of management qualifications. He has described them as a solution for the 19th century rather than one for the 1990s, looking forward to Britain in Europe . . . I find it curious that on the one hand Lord Young spends his time berating the professional institutes of the middle class for their restrictive practice tendencies and yet on the other hand he appears to be strongly behind these proposals.

The new age

The first wave of the Agricultural Revolution took 2000 years. The second wave of the Industrial Revolution took 200 years. The third wave of the Information Technology Revolution has taken 20 years. In order to survive this third wave, organizations will need to be fleet of foot and adapt quickly to changes in both the internal and external environment. John Sculley (1987) has suggested that because of the changes in the world, organizations need to move away from what he calls the *second wave form* to a *third wave form*. Table 12.1 illustrates the characteristics of these waves.

In a similar vein Tom Peters, author of *Thriving on chaos* (1988), has referred to the present time as the 'age of uncertainty. . . the technology revolution. . . the age of the gazelle. . . the

148

Table 12.1 Evolving into third wave forms

Characteristic	Second wave	Third wave
Organization	Hierarchy	Network
Output	Market share	Market creation
Focus	Institution	Individual
Style	Structured	Flexible
Source of strength	Stability	Change
Structure	Self-sufficiency	Interdependency
Mission	Goals, strategy	Identity, values
Leadership	Dogmatic	Inspirational
Quality	Affordable best	No compromise
Expectations	Security	Personal growth
Status	Title and rank	Creativity
Resource	Cash	Information
Advantage	Better sameness	Meaningfulness
Motivation	To complete	To build

Table 12.2 New age organizations

The past age of	The new age of
Pyramids	Alliances
Centralized	Decentralized
Top down	Bottom up
The boss	Self-management
Management	Autonomous worker action
Manuals and procedures	Visions and values

destruction of the hierarchy. . . the information age. . . the explosion of new competitors. . . the changing tastes of consumers'. To cope with this age, organizations need people who are 'entrepreneurs and champions, sprinters, coping with ambiguity and uncertainty, being opportunistic, change agents, managing themselves. . . being concerned with the product, flexibility, quality, service through a love of people'. Table 12.2 shows the way in which organizations are changing. Commenting on this age of uncertainty, Peters says:

This literally throws everything we have known into a cocked hat – the way we plan, the way we train, the way we execute and in particular, the way we empower front line people and turn them into strategists in the real sense of the term. What we need to worry about is quality, service, innovation, people, entrepreneurship, empowerment. My final comment on the list of needs is the absolute necessity for more entrepreneurship and smaller companies.

In the *Harvard Business Review* Peter Drucker (1988) says: 'The best example of a large and successful information based organization had no middle managers at all . . . Information based organizations . . . require clear, simple, common objectives that translate into particular actions.' He sees as 'particularly critical' the following priorities:

- developing rewards, recognition and career opportunities for specialists;
- creating unified vision in an organization of specialists;
- devising the management structure for an organization of task forces;
- ensuring the supply, preparation and testing of top management people.

He views the last priority as probably the toughest. 'We may also find that more and more top management jobs in big companies are filled by hiring people away from smaller companies. This is the way that major orchestras get their conductors – a young conductor earns his or her spurs in a small orchestra or opera house, only to be hired away by a larger one.'

The response in the UK

In this changing business environment, different demands are being placed on employees. As a consequence, the education system needs to change. Are schools concerned about developing empowered people who can be entrepreneurs, capable of coping with ambiguity and uncertainty? Are they producing individuals who are ready to be opportunistic, flexible, creative, inspirational and change agents? Will these individuals be capable of managing themselves, yet also show concern about quality and other people?

In a letter to *The Times*, Edward de Bono (1988) talks about the Education Reform Bill in Britain. He comments:

Schools have always concerned themselves with numeracy and literacy and that remains the preoccupation of the new Bill. Yet operacy (the skill of doing) is every bit as important – probably much more important for most youngsters. At best education does half its job, as it concerns itself with description, analysis and critical thinking, as if these were sufficient. The thinking of operacy is quite different and is concerned with objectives, priorities, values, alternatives, guessing, consequences, decisions, conflict and other people's views. There is now ample evidence to show that these things can be taught directly in school as part of the curriculum. More progressive countries are already doing this – USA, Canada, China, Venezuela, Bulgaria, Singapore, Malaysia, Australia – to various degrees.

During the last three years or so, Professor Hugh Murray, of the London based City University Business School, has strongly argued that MBAs are a US solution to a problem that we have never had in the UK. Murray sees the need for management education to move from narrow professionalism to broad generalist. He believes there are three dimensions to the process. These are:

- knowledge
- skills
- personal development.

Murray's emphasis is not on academic inputs but on managerial *outputs*. City's Consortium MBA approach, which consists of several businesses joining together to design a MBA course in collaboration with an educational institution, is based on individually tailored programmes for each student and focuses on three or four company-based assignments. The individual development required by each student is assessed by tests and questionnaires devised by Ronnie Lessem, a Reader in international management at City University Business School. He uses the same theoretical base as the *vision to action* model described below.

151

From vision to action

This model takes into account many of the points made above. It is concerned with 'operacy', energy, and the differences that exist in people and the roles and situations in which they are placed. It is concerned with self-development and has been very successfully used by the Urban and Economic Development Group (URBED) to develop budding entrepreneurs (over 2,000 people have been through their programmes).

The way in which it has been used by QUARTO to develop managers in large companies can be explained through the *Seven Ps*. These outline the stages involved in managing a vision or idea through to action.

1 *Developing the purpose*

For any project, assignment or business to be successful there needs to be a vision or an idea that defines the mission and the specific business objectives. This may be in words or in numbers. It can also be in terms of an all-embracing picture that becomes the 'obsession' that drives an entrepreneur on, despite all the difficulties that arise along the way.

Such a vision deals with the following issues:

- what business am I in?
- what do I want to create?
- what business should I be in?
- what is my chief aim or mission?
- how will this affect my life?

The outcome of this first activity is that the manager has a clear purpose with defined and specific, yet simple, objectives.

2 *Positioning: finding a fit or position in the market*

There needs to be a fit between the vision, skills and abilities of the manager, the resources available to him or her, and the customer and market needs. The following questions need to be asked:

- what particular market niche am I capable of filling?

- what are the signs of the times?
- who will buy, what will they buy and for how much?
- is the idea timely, in harmony with the environment, and likely to take seed and grow?

The outcome of this is that a match will be established between the market, the vision and the resources available to an organization.

3 *Planning: getting organized*

Once objectives are clear and harmony exists between the vision, market and resources, the next stage is to implement the idea. Managers need to decide:

- what needs to be done
- what major functions have to be performed in the business
- what the key tasks are to be done
- how they are going to be done
- who is going to be responsible for them
- where the resources are coming from.

The outcome of this is that policies, plans, systems, procedures and a structure (i.e. roles and relationships) are mapped out. Systems will bring order to the attainment of the vision.

4 *Power: making a commitment*

The time of commitment has arrived. In the light of the work that has been done so far, is the project viable? Relevant questions include:

- what are the risks of getting involved?
- is the project going to work?
- what financial reward do I want?
- what do I personally want to achieve?

The outcome of this stage is that resources are committed, and power and energy are mobilized to overcome any obstacles in the way of profitably achieving the vision and objectives of the organization.

5 Creating processes: planning in detail

The next step is to plan in detail what needs to be done and when to get things going. Managers should ask:

- what am I trying to achieve?
- how will I achieve it?
- who will do what and when?
- what is the cash flow, sales and profit forecast?
- are the proposed systems and procedures sufficient?

The outcome of this stage is that information has been gathered about internal and external strengths, weaknesses, opportunities and threats.

6 People: pulling people in and building alliances

This is the time to make contacts and allies, to recruit and motivate the staff to transform the vision into reality. Managers should ask:

- what are the key activities required?
- what job demands are going to be made?
- what skills are required to meet these demands?
- who are the key people to make it work?
- how will I meet their needs and motivate them?
- how do I find and make allies to cooperate with me?
- what attitudes and motivations shape the culture?

The outcome of this step is that a supportive culture has been developed with collaborative teamworking and shared values.

7 Products: getting going through producing or servicing

All the previous activities need to be completed satisfactorily for the action – whether in the form of a product or a service – to be both effective and efficient. Managers should now assess:

- what is occurring and is it appropriate and efficient?
- how do I best spend my time?
- whose skills are best spent on what activity?

154

● how do I develop, delegate and train staff?

The outcome of this step is that the resources to produce the product or service are operating efficiently.

Traits of entrepreneurial managers

Managing the process of taking a vision or idea through to action requires specific knowledge, skills and attitudes. A manager needs to be purposeful, positive and assertive. He or she needs confidence and self-esteem. In addition, each of the seven activities outlined requires different skills, styles and energies. However, each of us has certain skills and preferred ways of operating. It is therefore probably rare to find one person who can take an idea or vision through all these stages successfully.

The necessary skills at each stage include the following:

* developing a PURPOSE or vision requires inspiration, creativity, imagination and enthusiasm;
* POSITIONING and finding a fit require intuition, foresight and a perceptive sensitivity (e.g. to trends);
* PLANNING and getting organized require conceptualizing, planning and administration skills, the ability to organize and lead;
* EMPOWERING and making a commitment require an entrepreneurial attitude, will-power and drive;
* PROCESSING and planning in detail require an analytical mind capable of scheduling activities, yet flexible enough to adapt to any problems and issues that arise;
* pulling PEOPLE in requires enthusiasm, networking and high interpersonal skills;
* PRODUCING and getting going require physical energy, stamina and an adventurous mind.

Applications

The *Seven Ps* process of vision to action is being used by the departments of several major corporations, including IBM, Kodak

155

and the UK's Training Agency. It has been used with great success to establish an appropriate corporate and customer orientation in these business units. The process has also been used by some of these units as a framework for team building.

References

de Bono, E. (1988), Letter to *The Times*, 27 January.

Burgoyne, J. and Stuart, R. (1976), 'The nature, use and acquisition of managerial skills and other attributes', *Personnel Review*, vol 5, No. 4, Autumn.

Calvert-Durkin Associates, 'Spectral training', unpublished paper.

Drucker, P. (1988), 'The coming of the new organization', *Harvard Business Review*, January–February.

Handy, C. (1987), *The making of managers* (London: National Economic Development Office Books).

Hills, C., *Nuclear Evolution* (California: University of the Trees Press).

IPM Digest, July 1988.

Lessem, R. (1987a), *Intrapreneurship* (Wildwood House).

Lessem, R. (1987b), *The global business* (New Jersey: Prentice Hall).

Lorenz, K. (1988), *The Waning Humaneness* (London: Unwin Hyman).

Murray, H. (1988), 'Management education and the MBA: It's time for a rethink', paper give to the AMED, CMED, Economist Conference, op. cit.

Peters, T. J. and Whiteman, R. H. (1982), *In Search of Excellence* (New York Harper & Row).

Peters, T. (1988), *Thriving on Chaos* (London: Macmillan).

Sculley, J. (1987), *Odyssey: Pepsi to Apple* (London: Collins).

SECTION 3

Framing the picture: managing in turbulent times

Introduction

In this final Section, Ronnie Lessem (Chapter 13) looks at the fundamental issue underlying all the previous chapters – what sort of manager is needed in tomorrow's business world? Lessem has no doubt that the *adaptive* manager is the answer. He or she is flexible and innovative and is able to recognize the common strands of concepts, approaches and issues that run through all business disciplines.

However, management development has so far failed to develop adaptive systems of learning to create this new breed of manager. Instead, competency systems have tended to be mechanistic and inflexible. Generalized and fixed lists of attributes only create *analytical* managers, individuals with a specialized, fragmented view of management.

The answer, says Lessem, is to develop a spectrum of approaches that can be applied to a variety of situations. This should emphasize the links between the various managerial functions so that managers develop flexible and integrative perspectives. This will enable them to move freely within and between functions. As the first step towards developing adaptive learning, Lessem highlights the contrast between analytical and adaptive approaches in finance, marketing, operations, human resources and personnel management.

In the final chapter (Chapter 14), Ben Thompson-McCausland describes his personal vision of how organizations can release human potential and power. His vision is grounded in the belief that managers in the next decade will be driven by a need for fulfilment and that business success will depend on tapping into and harnessing this need.

Businesses will achieve this only by understanding the symbiotic relationship between the individual and the organization. Thompson-McCausland uses five conventional aspects of corporate life to illustrate this relationship. He then goes on to develop this link by exploring 'corporate energy' and the 'corporate mind'. Building on this symbiotic relationship, organizations can work towards mutual fulfilment. Such a partnership, Thompson-McCausland believes, will be the power propelling businesses forward in the 1990s.

CHAPTER 13

The adaptive manager

RONNIE LESSEM

Over the last decade managers have called for an adaptive approach to management. In other words, they have highlighted the necessity of managing within a changing environment. Ironically, while this clarion call has often been sounded, the substance of business and management theory has hardly changed over the last 30 years. More specifically, whereas there has been considerable theoretical adaptation in the fields of organizational behaviour and information technology, the changes in finance, operations, business policy and marketing have been few and far between.

For the sake of managerial balance I have deliberately set out in this chapter to develop an adaptive approach to business and management. Whereas the analytical approach is ready to hand, an adaptive one has still to be developed – particularly in the areas of marketing and business strategy.

Analytical approaches involve the design and application of generalized principles to cover management situations at any time and in any place. Adaptive approaches, in contrast, involve a spectrum of different approaches which are flexibly designed and applied to a variety of situations. It is this complementarity between analysis, associated with order and continuity, and adaptation, associated with freedom and discontinuity, that characterizes the European democratic and scientific spirit. By contrast the Western (American) and Eastern traditions, not to mention the South, are different.

Because management theory has failed to evolve – at least outside of America – managers in the 1980s often confuse enterprise and shared values (Tom Peters' buzz words) with adaptation and

161

change. In our restless urge to escape from 'paralysis by analysis' we have gone back to the 'primal' virtues of yesterday rather than forward to the rational requirements of tomorrow. In other words, drawing on current terminology, we have gone from maintenance or analytically based learning back to instinctive learning, rather than forward to innovative or adaptive learning. In the rest of this chapter, then, I shall reveal what this forward movement generally represents for the major functions of business, starting with financial management.

Financial management

Money and finance have never been very far apart. In fact, particularly for those who have not been involved in business themselves, the two may appear inextricably connected.

Money, though, is actually an abstraction. People who are instinctively adept at making it start out with a primal desire to achieve, to acquire and to possess, rather than a wish to analyse a balance sheet or profit and loss account. Analytically based financial management is in fact a rational progression from out of the 'primal' depths.

The foundations for such rationally based financial management were laid in seventeenth-century Italy, when double-entry book keeping was first invented.

Subsequent developments of the financial function, often mathematically based, have further extended its rationality. Discounted cash flow, capital budgeting, portfolio analysis and financial model building and simulation, have added degrees of intellectual sophistication to an already analytically refined discipline.

However, a combination of competitive instinct and intellectual wizardry, heightened by the internationalization of markets, has produced a financial revolution.

Adaptive finance

Walter Wriston, head of Citicorp, the world's largest bank, believes that between 1970 and 1984 'the information standard has replaced the gold standard as the basis for internal finance. Communications now enable and ensure that money moves anywhere around the

162

globe in answer to the latest information or misinformation. There now exists a new order, a global marketplace for ideas, money, goods and services that knows no national boundaries.'

An intellectual superstructure has been built directly upon a primal substructure, resulting in great fluidity and instability. Fixed and archaic primal instincts have become intwined with a flexible intellect, contained in both people and technology.

For generations, centuries in the case of many of the great financial capitals of the world, the principles guiding the financial markets have been specialization and control. The Chicago commodity markets concentrated on futures in pork bellies, the Baltic Exchange in London developed the markets for freight rates by sea. Markets for short, medium and long term funds were separated and the whole structure buttressed by central authorities that controlled interest rates and currency movements.

In the 1980s, however, technology has made it possible to trade huge volumes on screens and on the exchange floors. What is more, it has made it possible to develop increasingly sophisticated and complicated products such as options (when the investor takes out an option to buy or sell a share, bond or commodity at a future date), swaps (when the borrower can swap, for example, his fixed rate debt, raised in one country, with the floating rate debt raised by a company elsewhere).

In summary, as both investors and borrowers grow more sophisticated, so new products are developed that enable companies to swap their obligations, investors to convert their bonds into equity shares or different currencies and banks to take advantage of their spread of customers to organize flexible instruments that could be made short term or long term, moved into one currency or another, and switched from floating to fixed interest rate at will.

(Hamilton, 1986)

The shift from gold (through coin, paper money and credit) to information as a unit of exchange progressively removes finance from its primal origins. At the same time, the proliferation of flexible, financial instruments within an international context reflects an increasingly adaptive approach to financial management.

163

A multiplicity of flexible transactions have replaced a relative paucity of fixed ones. These range from 'systemic' offerings of combined hardware and software support to basic commodity trading. Moreover, it is the ability to switch rapidly from one to the other that characterizes adaptive financial management.

In the final analysis, information flows have overtaken gold stocks as an indicator of business and economic dynamism (although not stability). Moreover, the ability to provide a flexible portfolio of customized, exclusive or specialized goods and services characterizes the adaptive financial organization. Such an adaptive organization not only anticipates transactional shifts over time but also participates in such shifts across local, national and international space.

Marketing management

While business is generally identified with money and finance, its origins lie closer to marketing. As Peter Drucker has emphasized: 'The purpose of a business is not to make a profit . . . Rather a business exists for its economic contribution. Its purpose is to create a customer.'

At the turn of the century, larger than life characters, such as 'King Gillette' in America, created products that they virtually willed into existence. Such individuals followed hunches, took breathtaking chances and finally conquered the world through their determination to succeed. They had charisma and a buccaneering style. Their business talents were as much instinctive as academic.

> Modern marketing man is different. Charisma? He thinks charisma is an Indian restaurant in suburbia. Buccaneering? That is in old black and white movies on TV. Modern marketing man is often dull, studious, careful, safe. He does everything by the book. But although this type doesn't get my adrenalin flowing, I won't condemn him out of hand.
>
> Big business is now exceedingly complex; there is a compelling need for high volume sales, and the degree of competition is so keen that only the most economical methods of design and production, or distribution, will maintain profitability.

It is therefore blindingly obvious that marketing – as it is now understood – embraces a whole lot more than simply selling the product. It must identify what product should be made, how, when and where it should be sold, how much it should be sold for and to whom?

(Turner, 1985)

For Harry Turner the 'modern marketeer' is an analyst of the 1950s and 1960s rather than an adaptive manager of the 1980s and 1990s. The high priest of such analytically based marketing is the American academic, Philip Kotler. He asserts: 'Marketing is the analyzing, organizing, planning and controlling of the firm's customer – impinging resources, policies and activities with a view to satisfying the needs and wants of chosen customer groups at a profit.'

As we can see, the abstract world of resources and customer groups replaces the concrete world of people and things. Figure 13.1 shows how the new science of analytical marketing was diagrammatically represented in the 1960s. Analytically based management has come a long way from its primal origins. It has substituted analytical cut and thrust for the emotionally based ego drive. In fact, by the 1970s marketing had become the most intellectually demanding of the business disciplines.

Cultural and social
environment

PRODUCT   PLACE

Political and   Resources and
legal environment   objectives of the firm

PRICE   PROMOTION

Economic   Existing
environment   business situation

Figure 13.1   The marketing manager's framework

Adaptive marketing

Kotler's approach to analytical marketing remained undisputed within the mainstream of corporate life until well into the 1980s.

165

Just recently, however, a new marketing orthodoxy has begun to emerge. This is equally rational but more flexible in its approach. Not surprisingly, its advocates are Western rather than Central European in origin. In fact it was the Dutchman, Bernard Lievegoed (1973), who conceived of 'relations management' in the early 1970s. Through this activity Lievegoed supplanted marketing and personnel management by relating to both employees and customers.

The 'Nordic School of Services', based in Finland and Sweden, has gone a step further. This has replaced the old concept of analytical marketing with a new 'interactive' one.

> Marketing can be seen as relationship management: creating, developing and maintaining a network in which the firm thrives. Such a network is interactive, that is involving bilateral and multilateral supplier-customer relationships, to produce goods and services. These relationships, finally, are long term, stressing that relationships need time to be built and to be maintained.
>
> (Gummesson, 1987)

The interactive approach to marketing, then, stresses building relationships rather than promoting products or satisfying individual customer needs. Moreover, these relationships extend beyond customers to suppliers, distributors and investors. A company can be viewed as a node in an ever widening pattern of interactions, in some of which it is a direct participant, some of which affect it indirectly and some of which occur independently of it.

As we can see, under the guise of 'relationships' and 'synergistic' marketing there is a full array of transactions, particularly of a customized (old friend), exclusive (long-term contract) and systemic (joint research and development) nature. This ability to adapt from one transaction to the other over time and across space differentiates adaptive from analytical marketing.

Operations management

Production and operations management is the poor relation of the business functions in America and Great Britain. On the one hand it is considered too close to engineering to be a business discipline

166

in its own right. On the other hand, it has become too mathematical to be accessible to the average manager or business student.

However, the emergence of communications technology in the past ten years has given operations management, together with so-called management services (computers and data processing), a new lease of life. Equally important has been the development of product quality.

The major vehicle for maintaining quality production in Japan has been the 'quality circle'. Interestingly enough, rationally based techniques for quality control were imported from America after the war. These were combined with primal Japanese features into a unique form.

Kagu Ishikawa, a Japanese production engineer who has written a book on the subject, defines the quality circle as 'a small group performing quality control activities voluntarily within the same workshop, carrying on continuously as part of a company wide programme, focusing on mutual development with all members participating'. The basic aims of quality control, Ishikawa says, are to:

- contribute to the improvement of the enterprise
- build up a 'worth-living-in', happy and bright workshop
- exercise human capacities fully.

Ishikawa has an interesting way of looking at management as a whole, which in many ways represents a primal approach to operations management. It contains the following three aspects:

People
The first concern of management is the happiness of the people who are connected with it. If the people – employees, subcontractors, consumers – do not feel happy and cannot be made happy, the company does not deserve to exist.

Quality
Defective products will not only inconvenience consumers but also hinder sales. If a company makes too many products that cannot be sold, it will waste raw materials and energy. This waste will be a loss for society. A company must always supply products with the qualities the consumer demands.

The photofit manager

Price, cost and profit
The consumer's main demand is for 'just quality at a just price'. No matter how inexpensive a product, no one will buy it if its quality is poor.

Analytical operations

Although Ishikawa has partially begun to move into rational management, the tone changes completely once we wholly get there. As Ray Wild, probably the best-known professor of operations management in the UK, puts it: 'An operating system is a configuration of resources combined for the provision of goods or services.' (1980)

> Bus and taxi services, motels and dentists, tailors and mines, fire services and refuse removers, retail organizations, hospitals and building contractors are all operating systems.
> They all, in effect, convert inputs in order to provide outputs that are required by a customer.
> Physical inputs will normally predominate, hence: operating systems convert, using physical resources, to create outputs, the function of which is to satisfy consumer wants, that is to provide some utility for the customer.
>
> (Wild, 1980)

The bulk of any operations management text contains mathematical and statistical techniques for such functions as facilities location and material handling, work study and measurement, activity and project scheduling, and inventory control. However, a rationally based and qualitative logic underlies it all. This can be divided between overall function and structure. The following four principal functions can be identified:

- *Manufacture*, where something is physically created. Process or mass production involves the continuous manufacture of a commodity in bulk. Batch production occurs where the number of discrete items to be manufactured is insufficient to enable mass production. Finally, jobbing manufacture is intermittent.

168

- *Transport*, through which the location of someone or something is physically moved, within or without the organization.
- *Supply*, through which the ownership or possession of an item is physically changed.
- *Service*, where something or someone is treated or accommodated.

The nature of the operations manager's job will to some extent depend on the nature of the system he or she is managing, albeit in a rational context. All such systems may be seen to comprise inputs, processes and outputs, as illustrated in Table 13.1.

Table 13.1 A simple operations system

INPUTS	PROCESS Function, i.e. manufacture, transport, supply, service	OUTPUTS
Materials Machines		Goods Services

This basic analytical model underlies the 'hard' and rational approach to operations management. In the last five years, in the wake of what the late Bill Abernathy at Harvard called an 'Industrial Renaissance' in America, a softer approach has emerged.

Adaptive operations

Abernathy and his production-minded colleagues at the Harvard Business School have called for the kind of renaissance in manufacturing technology that effectively 'de-matures' such large and mature companies as General Motors and General Electric. With a different view of maturity from the one adopted in this text, Abernathy calls for technology-based revitalization of large-scale manufacturing enterprise. In the process he exposes the limitations of the conventionally analytical approach to operations.

Our task is to incorporate particular new technologies and heightened product variety into high volume manufacturing systems and to do so without the luxury of long lead times.

What is therefore needed is a view of production as an enterprise of unlimited potential, an enterprise in which current arrangements [as those set out above by Wild] are but the starting point for continuous organizational learning. No omniscient engineer ever handed down a design for product or production that could not stand improvement.

We do not mean, of course, that learning should proceed while schedules and shipping deadlines get ignored; competent management requires simultaneous attention to both current tasks and future possibilities. What gets lost in the shuffle, however, is the intimate connection between the two.

Only when grafted on to a production system dedicated to ongoing learning and communication, only when used in tandem with a skilled and responsible workforce, can new technologies realize their potential as competitive weapons. Only when such a workforce is truly engaged in the enterprise and encouraged to learn and excel, can a company hope to introduce competitively successful new products in a timely fashion.

(Abernathy, Clark and Kantrow, 1983)

The 'Industrial Renaissance' takes America, if not other nations, a long way from the world of machines, materials and labour towards one where 'human capital' working through information technology will make the difference between success and failure. In fact Koji Kobayashi, Chairman of NEC, the Japanese semiconductor company, makes a similar point: 'In order to respond to the shift from mass orientation toward product diversity and individuality, and to meet a wider variety of customer needs, very large amounts of information will need to be generated. The transfer and processing of the information, moreover, will be done at the plant.'

A new vocabulary has emerged. Programmable automation permits an automated machine to perform a range of tasks. This permits a single range of equipment to produce a variety of

170

components or to assemble a variety of products, creating flexibility. Economies of scope stand alongside economies of scale.

(Cohen and Zysman, 1987)

As such, adaptively based economies of scope overtake analytically based economies of scale. As a result, the transactional base shifts. Instead of a predominance of standardized and specialized offerings, we have a combination of systemic, exclusive, specialized, customized, consultancy-based crafts and commodities such as goods and services. What of the implications, then, for human resource management?

Human resource management

Elements of the 'human resource' function began to appear in Europe and America at the turn of the century. This was in reaction to the harsh behaviour of autocratic businessmen like Henry Ford! It was not until the 1940s and 1950s that, like most other business disciplines, it began to acquire fuller shape and form.

In fact, owing to its peculiar origins – a reaction against unscrupulous entrepreneurial behaviour – 'personnel' missed out on its instinctual origins. It was not until the redoubtable Peters and Waterman appeared on the primal scene, almost 20 years later, that the penny began to drop. 'Business is people' (either in the shape of employees or as customers and suppliers) was the primal conclusion. There was both a tough and a tender approach to this argument.

Ironically, many human resource managers are not innately 'people' oriented. This is because they are cut off from their childlike, instinctive selves. In other words they have grown up, and become rational!

Analytical personnel management

In the early days of management's evolution, attempts to rationalize production and organization were tentative and *ad hoc*. However, in the first decades of the twentieth century, businessmen did come under the influence of engineers. Such 'social engineers' sought to substitute rational 'scientific management' for the highly personalized, idiosyncratic style of the owner manager.

Some of the earliest efforts at substituting rational procedures for intuition and family traditions simply involved better record keeping, for which purpose many personnel departments were first established. Personnel records included details about when the employee was hired, educational background and succession of jobs, and also provided a record of time and production for payrolls. These were relatively routine clerical tasks.

This concern with methods was a precursor of personnel's current concern with training. It also represented an irrevocable and powerful drive towards increasing specialization.

INDUSTRIAL PSYCHOLOGY

In the late 1920s, rationalization and efficiency were the watchwords. The need to rationalize production arose from the new kinds of problems created by competition and demand and inventions in machinery and techniques.

Many jobs were broken down. In order to rationalize manufacturing amalgamations took place. Planning and efficiency in all aspects of a business became essential. Rationalization brought complexity with it. Selection assumed increasing importance during the 1920s because of the requirements of efficiency and the demands of complexity. As a result of government experience of classifying recruits during the First World War, psychologists were brought into industry to help pick out the most able workers. They developed testing techniques for assessing individual differences and personnel began concentrating on selection methods.

INDUSTRIAL RELATIONS

The influence of personnel expanded during the 1930s and 1940s. With their title changed to industrial relations, many personnel departments began to take charge of hiring, firing, wage determination, handling union grievances and deciding who should be transferred and promoted.

The personnel department suddenly gained much power, partly because of management's widespread recognition of the importance of the human element, but chiefly because of the threat of unionism. Personnel managers were now called on to be negotiators, drawing on tough primal qualities of stamina and risk taking. Unfortunately, the industrial relations manager's foe was not the external competition but the internal labour force.

PROFESSIONALIZATION

By the end of the Second World War, the functions of a personnel department could be clearly differentiated between employment, wages, joint consultation, health and safety, and education and training. By 1939 the perception of the range of personnel activities was fairly clear to the boards of larger, more highly organized companies. However, the specialist sectors of the work were not always well coordinated.

All this resulted in a much fuller functioning of human resource management. Within a few years half a dozen of its component parts were distinguished, each with its own distinct theory and skills. Recruitment, training, performance appraisal, industrial relations and personnel administration became sub-disciplines in their own right. As a profession, human resource management was coming of age.

HUMAN RELATIONS

By the 1950s and 1960s human resource management was seen to be relevant to the whole work situation. It addressed the interrelationship between the work to be done, the individuals and the groups carrying it out, and the environment in which the whole activity took place.

A new phase of professionalism began in the middle 1950s. Specialists developed certain elements of personnel management in depth and identified new approaches with the help of the social sciences. Of course, the application of sociology and psychology to the management of organizations had been initiated in the USA during the 1920s and 1930s by Mary Parker Follett, Elton Mayo and Chester Barnard.

Adaptive personnel management

The origins of what came to be called 'organization development' lie in the 1950s, when the then director of the Institute of Personnel Management was beginning to identify two distinct aspects of the personnel function. As he said at a European personnel conference in 1956:

> On the one hand, there are the processes of analysing the existing conditions and resources in the light of the requirements of the enterprise, of diagnosing and defining its problems, of prescribing and executing the appropriate action to bring about change. This may be regarded as a predominantly creative and dynamic aspect.
>
> On the other hand, there are the routine administrative duties involved in the execution of established policy, the solution of minor problems as they occur, the maintenance of healthy relationships, and the provision of personnel services.

As Warren Bennis said in the 1960s: 'Bureaucracy was a monumental discovery for harnessing muscle power via guilt and instinctual renunciation. In today's world it is a prosthetic device, no longer useful. For we now require organic–adaptive systems as structures of freedom to permit the expression of play and imagination and to exploit the new pleasures of work.' Some large companies, such as Texas Instruments in the US and ICI in Britain, tried to introduce Bennis' ideas in the 1960s and 1970s. However, these early attempts were often only halfhearted, partly because organization development had not yet come of age.

In the meanwhile, some very interesting developmental work was going on in Holland during the 1970s. This was led by the social psychologist, Bernard Lievegoed. His book *The Developing Organization* has influenced many managers because he has a much more thorough understanding of development than his better-known American counterparts. We glibly talk about personal, organization or business development and yet few of us are familiar with the intrinsic nature of it. Development is qualitative, discontinuous, irreversible, interspersed with evolutionary crises and 'dynamical balances'. Good human resource managers and organization developers need to be able to work consciously within such an evolutionary framework. This approach leads in two directions, one vertically towards manager self-development, and the other horizontally towards organizational harmony.

174

The subject of self-development has become very popular in personnel circles. In most cases, however, no more than lip service is paid to development. The idea that a manager should take responsibility for his or her own learning is built into personnel, but no conscious path of development is established.

On the other hand, an evolutionary perspective was built into Abraham Maslow's work some 20 years ago when he traced a personal and managerial path towards self-actualization through a hierarchy of needs. More recently, Daniel Levinson (1986) has indicated in *The seasons of a man's life* that we evolve through alternating structure-building and structure-changing phases during our life span. In my own work on *Intrapreneurship* I have related seven kinds of individuality to the four structure-building phases – youth, adulthood, midlife and maturity. Each intrapreneur or individual manager, in the terms of this text, develops in a unique way but passes through similar phases and transitions.

A developing organization, then, not only consciously enables individuals within it to grow but also evolves in itself. Vertical development, whereby one stage is interwoven with the other over time, is accompanied by horizontal development, where one part of the organization is interwoven with the other across space. During such integration, the protective membranes isolating one function or business from the other are broken down and re-formed into open filters. An exchange of energy between personnel and marketing, or between human resources and information technology, thus becomes possible. Each becomes a part of a continually re-emerging whole.

In the US, finally, a whole new school of thought has developed around corporate culture. This focuses on organizational transformation (OT) as opposed to organizational development (OD). This new thinking concentrates not on individuals and groups but on myths and rituals, emerging out of the historical depths of an organization's being. The emergence of corporate culture and of 'spirit' as a new field of management concern is a reflection of this metaphysical aspect of personnel management.

Myths are the stories of a group's culture which describe its beginning, continuance and ultimate goals. These stories are so much part of that fabric as to define that fabric and institution.

To know the myth is to know the institution in a way that balance sheets and organization charts can never report.

I view ritual as the dramatic re-enactment of a myth. In a ritual, the group acts out the central stories in such a way that the members experience really being there and participating in the original event.

The role of myths and rituals in organization transformation is critical, for they shape and form the culture, which in turn provides the power, purpose and values of the organization. The focus of development in the high performing frame of reference is on continuing transformation and renewal.

(Owen, 1987)

Within business circles in Europe and the US, corporate culture has displaced management style and organizational behaviour as the prevailing concern of progressive human resource managers. The language of myth and ritual, of beliefs and values, and of stories and heroism, has taken over from the more rationally based 'interpersonal' or 'socio-technical processes'. As a result, transactions within and between people and organizations extend not only from the technical to the social, and from the physical to the economic, but also from the cultural to the religious. Adaptive organizations need to provide individuals with 'spiritual' as well as economic and social sustenance. Adaptive personnel managers, therefore, are able to switch from one kind of psychological transaction to another as and when required.

Conclusion

Unlike his or her more specialized but less flexible analytical counterpart, the adaptive manager can adapt psychologically and/or commercially to diverse sets of people, organizations, marketplaces or whole societies. Some of these responses are illustrated in Table 13.2.

While analytical managers are specialists in financial marketing, operations or personnel management, adaptive managers are not generalists in the normal sense of the word. They are adapters. They are either able to switch transactions vertically within a function or,

176

if they attain managerial mastery, able to switch horizontally between functions. In summary, compared with their analytical counterparts, what adaptive managers lose in depth, they gain in height and breadth.

Table 13.2 Adaptive transactions

Managerial attribute	Financial management	Marketing management	Operations management	Personnel management
Energy				Ergonomics
Enthusiasm			Quality	Circles
Flexibility	Flexible instruments	Relationships marketing	Flexible manufacture	Planning for change
Enterprise	Trading	Salesmanship	Intrapreneur-ing	
Analysis	Management accounting	Analytical marketing	Analytical operations	Human resource management
Insight		Synergistic marketing		Organization development
Imagination				Organization transformation

References

Abernathy, W. (1983), *Industrial renaissance* (Oxford: Basil Books).

Cohen, S. and Zysman, I. (1987), *Manufacturing matters* (Oxford: Basil Books).

Gummesson, E. (1987), The new marketing, *Long Range Planning*, Vol. 20, No. 4.

Hamilton, A. (1986), *The financial revolution* (London: Viking).

Ishikawa, K. (1985), *What is total quality control?* (New Jersey: Prentis Hall).

Levinson, D. (1978), *Seasons of a man's life* (Knorf).

Lievegoed, B. C. J. (1973), *The developing organization* (Tavistock).

Owen, H. (1987), *Spirit, transformation and development* (Abbott).

Turner, H. (1985), *The gentle art of salesmanship* (London: Fontana).

Wild, R. (1980), *Essentials of operations management* (Holt Business Texts).

CHAPTER 14

In search of fulfilment

BEN THOMPSON-McCAUSLAND

In this chapter I have tried to deal with what I regard as the main need for management in the next decade. I am afraid this need is not concerned with processes or techniques in any particular way. It deals rather imprecisely with the symbiotic relationship between the individual and the corporation. It contains quite a large number of sweeping statements, which I trust are linked together in something like a logical sequence. I know that I am guilty of throwing in from time to time a good number of asides. The chapter certainly lacks elegance but this quality is not always a priority in business. Effectiveness is, however, a priority. If what I say is in any way controversial, then so much the better. The aim is to present concepts and ideas that are directly or indirectly linked to personal fulfilment at work.

I would like to start with a very sweeping statement which can be easily challenged. This is that the real need of management in the 1990s will be fulfilment. I am going to defend this statement by taking five conventional aspects of corporate life, namely planning, resources, shared values, change and teamwork. I will use these dimensions to illustrate the interrelationship between the individual's need for fulfilment and the corporation. To these I would like to add two rather unconventional aspects, namely corporate energy and the corporate mind.

Planning

To start with planning, the need for this will undoubtedly increase in the 1990s. In case that thought sends frissons of anxiety down the spines of those who secretly fear planning, let me say that I have learned that planning must be widely owned. It has to be alive, it has to be stretching, it must be ambitious and fresh. It seems to me that planners lapse into over-complication and the result is that many potential planners (and we are all potential planners) are put off before they even start. This means they never even get round to planning for their own personal fulfilment.

If planning is permitted to become mechanistic, boring or bureaucratic, fulfilment will not be achieved. Once planning becomes boring, it stops being planning and just becomes a ritual. It effectively hinders or discourages any sort of fulfilment. Disciplined monitoring is, of course, absolutely essential. Although it carries within itself the seeds of bureaucracy, it has still to be carried through. Without disciplined monitoring, planning can and does lapse into charismatic but deceptive exhortation. Although it may focus energy quite sharply, perhaps even spectacularly, it often fails to channel it effectively. In other words, fulfilment in those circumstances can be intense but unsustainable and seems to be followed invariably by frustration. What we are seeking is continuous fulfilment.

To sum up, planning is either fun or boring; it is either enthusiastic or lifeless; it is either innovative or ritualistic; it is either energizing or lethargic. These things, I believe, apply just as much to personal planning as they do to corporate planning.

Resources

This brings us to resources. People are far and away the most important corporate resource and they will remain so. However, they are no more than this. When keenly endeavouring to develop people and to care for them, it is very easy to forget that the needs of the business must come first. None the less, this fulfilment is essential, not just because people are important and possess literally inestimable talent but because this talent needs, even craves, fulfilment. No organization can improve continuously unless it is committed to identifying, encouraging and using that talent.

This concern with fulfilment is not a soft process. Talent needs to be stretched and people do not always want to be stretched. Indeed, fulfilment of individual talent can often be uncomfortable. However, I suspect that we quite often confuse comfort with what we think is right and discomfort with what we are quite certain is wrong.

Collectively, the process of fulfilling individual talent gives rise to what could be described as corporate energy. This in turn has to be controlled if it is not to be fruitlessly squandered. The word 'control' may sound slightly repressive, but this really means engaging as opposed to wasting energy. The purpose of control, after all, is not to thwart but to increase effectiveness.

I believe that the correct fulfilment of human talent within a corporate environment should lead to consistently sound financial results. Financial results themselves should be seen primarily as a measure of the effective use of resources, as opposed to the expedient juggling of figures for short-term year-end purposes.

Shared values

If we are to use our human resources to produce continually improving results in the 1990s, companies need to consider shared values. My personal definition of shared values is that they are the core beliefs about a company to which we can unhesitatingly give our talent and our energy. To do this unhesitatingly requires commitment born of conviction.

Without conscious shared values, we cannot expect to harness the potential of people working within the organization. There will always be some sort of holding back, a lack of total commitment. Shared values are a means of underpinning improvement and bringing about lasting change instead of superficial change. They can provide opportunity for personal fulfilment. Through shared values, management develops both individually and corporately. However, every effort to establish and use shared values will disintegrate without continuous and visible commitment from the top.

Defining shared values and gaining widespread agreement about them may seem a tough process. However, in my experience, that difficulty pales into insignificance when compared with the responsibility of sustaining them or living up to them. They require understanding, even forgiveness. That is because they bring us face to face with our own personal limitations. Such confrontations call for quite high levels of moral courage because there are never any escape routes.

To survive, shared values need a secure and respected process, which has to be planned. Shared values enable us to deal with change, of which there will be a great deal in the 1990s.

Change

Whether we like it or not, change is with us. Moreover, we are not changing from one steady state to another steady state, such as was enjoyed in the 1950s through to most of the 1970s. We are changing to yet more change. However, if companies are to make any headway they need to change more rapidly than their markets. Herein lies a dilemma because the reality of change in corporations is that it actually happens much more slowly than management would like to think. Managers desire change and they actually have a duty to implement it. Through wishful thinking, however, we often confuse superficial change with the real thing. This can lead to discouragement and disillusionment, the reverse of fulfilment.

Teamwork

Teamwork occurs only when the corporate energy of an organization is effectively engaged. Whether or not teamwork brings about the effective use of that corporate energy is difficult to judge and is perhaps not that important to practising managers.

Corporate energy

Very little has been written about the concept of corporate energy yet I believe it exists in every organization. It can be very easily dispersed, it can go underground, but it cannot be destroyed.

Companies that are in touch with their corporate energy and that strive to get closer to it pave the way to personal fulfilment for their

181

people. I suggest that corporate energy is the common factor in all high-performing companies. Planning, development of resources, sharing of values and teamwork are the component parts of the equipment needed to tap into that corporate energy.

Corporate energy is a force. In organizations where attempts have been made to tap it, the force can easily be felt or experienced by the first-time visitor. Equally, where corporate energy is untapped, it is all too easy to perceive its lack. It is an energizing and fulfilling experience to work with a company that is in touch with its corporate energy and conversely it is a slog trying to work with companies disconnected from their energy.

Corporate energy can lead to corporate miracles, or at least near miracles, but it is hard to harness and it needs control. It will evaporate uselessly if negative qualities are tolerated in companies. These include selfishness; corporate sloth or complacency; poor communication or obsession with status; lack of fulfilment; refusal to work together and any form of segmentalism. These things are clearly inimical to fulfilment.

Most people recognize that they can achieve very little in organizations through their own efforts alone. However, helping to create an environment where everyone wishes to contribute can result in a total effort that seems many times more powerful than the sum of the parts. This is corporate energy at work. But how do we actually find such corporate energy and then unleash it? Having achieved this, how do we harness it?

We have to appreciate that the characteristics of corporate energy vary from company to company. What counts is not the manifestation of the energy but rather the effectiveness of its application. Every company has its own corporate energy, corporate values (whether conscious or not), experience, rhythm and its own opportunities to produce fulfilment.

In the next decade, managers will increasingly need to listen to those things and to gauge them in order to be able to work with them. But all too often, heavily conditioned or armed with inadequately understood theories, we try and change those things. We fail to recognize them for what they are. We have the same effect as a policeman on traffic duty at a roundabout in the rush hour – we stop the natural tendency of people to act and think intelligently. The result is that the blockage becomes intensified. However, no single manager ever really believes himself or herself guilty of this. In fact, everyone is. Managers would do well at appraisals to invite subordinates or appraisees to tell them when and how they get in the way and block fulfilment.

The corporate mind

These thoughts, and particularly the interaction of the corporate values, rhythm and corporate energy, can be illustrated by using the concept of the 'corporate mind'. Parallels with the human brain can be drawn in that both have hemispheres but, instead of a left and right hemisphere, the corporate mind can be thought of as having a positive hemisphere and a negative hemisphere.

What drives the corporate mind is the brains, the experience, the effort, the values and the rhythm of the people working within the corporation. Every group has its own ethos, its own personality or, in other words, its own corporate mind. The character of this mind is moulded by the influences projected by its individual members. Corporate personality begins to form from the moment the group is first assembled. It continues to grow until, at its most advanced stage, it produces quite exceptional teams. But if the negative hemisphere is allowed to dominate, the results can be dismal.

The positive hemisphere

The positive hemisphere of the corporate mind is the part that signals 'WE CAN' in response to any challenge or objective. The most important parts of this hemisphere are confidence, energy and teamwork.

Confidence does not need to be mentioned, except to note that 'we can' signals, when channelled to this part of the corporate mind, generally end up in a subdivision of confidence that can be called determination. Thus, in respect of the corporate objective, the corporate mind will signal not only that we can but that 'we will'. However, without the help of other parts of the positive section of the corporate mind, notably energy and teamwork, confidence and determination remain nothing but an empty corporate fantasy.

As already indicated, teamwork is clearly important if a corporation is to realize the positive intentions that are sparked off within
the corporate mind. Here the essential nature of trust needs to be
acknowledged. Trust is not something that businesses can actually
command. No executive, however powerful, can guarantee that he
or she will be trusted simply because he or she demands to be.
Subordinates are free to give or withhold trust just as they want.
Those who would have the trust of their colleagues can obtain it
only by helping create an environment in which trust will grow
more or less of its own accord. If the required environment is to
be developed or, perhaps more accurately, if it is to develop itself,
the manager or leader obviously has to display integrity. Without
this, trust will be an uncertain thing.

Given an acceptable level of integrity, it is still by no means
certain that true teamwork will actually develop. There has to
be a minimum degree of understanding between each member
of the team or group. The strengths and weaknesses, actions and
reactions of each member must be understood by each of his or
her colleagues. This will enable each one of them to know as if by
instinct how the team will react in given circumstances and how
the circumstances will affect each team member.

If it is accepted that corporate objectives are to be achieved
through teamwork and not by the efforts of a single star performer,
it follows that each individual must subordinate his or her desire
for immediate personal fulfilment to the greater objective of group
achievement. To make a sacrifice like this, the individual has to be
convinced that the group objective is more important. Without that
conviction, he or she will find it hard to see problems through other
eyes. The ability to do this is an essential ingredient of teamwork. It
can be called humility and is often needed when conditions are at
their most difficult or fraught.

Teamwork requires a high level of communicating ability. Unfortunately people tend to assume that they can communicate just
because they can read, write, telephone or tap keys on a computer
terminal. Far from it. Communication is probably one of the
most difficult tasks of management, despite proven experience
that people will accept an enormous amount of 'how' if only
managers will tell them 'why'. Far greater communicating abilities
will be needed in the next decade. People will need to communicate

their true feelings to their teams in an environment of trust (which of course calls for courage).

The negative hemisphere

If corporations were driven solely by their positive hemispheres, they would be capable of miracles. Unfortunately, however, we have to deal with the existence of the negative hemisphere, which keeps us firmly earth-bound. The negative hemisphere can never be eliminated. All management can do is to take steps to reduce its effect.

Unless properly controlled, the negative hemisphere can paralyse the good effect of the positive hemisphere. Just as the automatic reaction of the positive hemisphere to any challenge is 'we can', so the reaction of the negative hemisphere is 'we can't'. It does not take many people, particularly key people, within an organization to signal in this way before the corporation begins to slip into some kind of negative drift. When this happens, the efforts of the management to direct and steer the company through the problems and blockages of the marketplace become ineffective. The response to management control becomes steadily more sluggish. A point may be reached where the company, weighed down with inertia, simply drifts before market forces.

Like the positive hemisphere, the negative hemisphere can be thought of as having three main compartments. The first of these can be called complacency. Into this area flow signals associated with administrative weakness – dependency; an inability to inspire, develop or lead.

The second area can be broadly described as the field of inertia. This leads to acquiescence, to unchecked inefficiency and to blindness to opportunity. It is here that the corporate equivalent of sloth has its source and also, I suspect, needless bureaucracy.

The third part of the negative hemisphere is selfishness. This area emanates signals like 'information is power, don't let anybody else have it'. Refusal to share means refusal to develop. It also means discarding opportunities to refine and perfect ideas.

In order for the corporate mind to work efficiently the members of staff have to have an actual or latent desire for the corporation to succeed. This desire cannot be imposed by management; no

185

person can force another person to desire. As in the case of trust, all management can do is to help create an environment in which the desire to succeed will grow naturally of its own accord.

We must again return to the need to identify and work with, not against, the positive hemisphere and its corporate rhythm. We must also return to the individual whom we left struggling a moment ago to share his or her true feelings with a team. Courageous sharing has a lot to do with the working of the corporate mind. The energies that it releases may be helpful, not only in planning but whenever a team experiences a significant loss of momentum or confidence.

If business opportunities are undertaken in an atmosphere of trust and the fear of destructive criticism has been totally removed, the interest of participants will be engaged. This will release their energy and excitement. The second stage is when concepts may be transformed into possibilities and even into probabilities. The real world breaks through in the third stage. Doubts occur and risks, which had previously been sublimated by enthusiasm, assume a harder focus.

People who have for one reason or another been unable to identify with stages 1 and 2 may have a much greater say at this point. After all, if you are a negative type of person, why waste criticism in stages 1 and 2 when you can have ten times the effect in stage 3? This stage can prove too much for those whose previous contributions had been based on nothing sounder than exhilaration or other undefined good feelings. The resulting anxiety and loss of confidence can lead to cynicism and defeatism.

In the fourth stage, uncertainty and perhaps even despondency or cynicism from stage 3 can be resolved through sharing of hopes, aims and doubts (there is nothing un-macho about sharing doubts) with trusted members of the team. This process should be able to restore proper balance and perspective.

This in turn gives rise to stage 5, renewed confidence. This confidence is not only restored but strengthened, ready to return to stage 1. This time, however, the team has advanced beyond the initial starting point. The process is not a circle but rather a spiral. Of the five stages in the spiral, the transition between stages 3 and 4 is the one that most tests individuals' courage and humility. It is therefore not very surprising that it is here where the spiral is most often broken. The negative side of the corporate mind is particularly influential because as teams repeatedly progress through the spiral, stage 3 becomes progressively more challenging.

Conclusion

Each person has literally inestimable talent and the employment of this talent leads to fulfilment. Talent is only rarely tapped in organizations because companies seldom succeed in surmounting the blockages along the way. Sometimes they find ways round through learning theories and techniques, but these will not really help unless they truly find an outlet for talent.

However, organizations have an opportunity to release talent through the positive hemispheres of their corporate minds. Personal talent can be linked to corporate talent through sharing. This requires courage because the negative hemisphere is hostile to the exercising of any talent. This hostility can be overcome by courageous sharing in an environment of trust. Sharing means contribution, which leads to the fulfilment of talent.

The real need for managers in the 1990s is to gain fulfilment. They need to recognize that they must find this not only for themselves but also, and most importantly, for those for whom they are responsible. Shared fulfilment is going to provide the power to propel organizations towards their corporate objectives in the 1990s.

Note

This chapter is based on a speech given at the Association for Management Education and Development conference *Management profiles for the 1990s*, 4-5 January 1989.

Index

Index

IBM 155
ICI 69, 90–9, 174
Incomes Data Services 62
individuals, and the organization 159
industrial psychology 172
industrial relations 172–3
Industrial Renaissance 170
Industrial Revolution 148
inertia 185
information, as financial standard 162–4
information technology 170
Information Technology Revolution 148–50
INSEAD 74
Institute of Manpower Studies 9, 11, 12, 13, 17
Institute of Personnel Management 173
integrated stage, organizational growth 112–13
integrators 2
intention stage, decision-making 142, 143
interactive marketing 166
internationalization, business 2, 35–6, 102
INTERPLACE 57, 60, 64
interviews
  action profiling 142
  situational 76–7, 82
involvement
  management teams 143–4
  teamworkers 145–6
Ishikawa, Kagu 167–8

Jacobs, Robin 9–10, 27, 39
Japan 147, 148
Jay, Anthony 56
job requirement exercise 60–1, 64
jobs, particular competences 106

Kantrow 170
knowledge, forms of 4
Kobayashi, Koji 170
Kodak 71, 155
Kotler, Philip 164–5

Lancaster University 74
leaders
  creating 91–2
  dealing with uncertainty 79–80
  identification in advance 72, 73
leadership 91
  bureaucratic organizations 131
  expert organizations 134
  link with personal power 69
  networking organizations 134–5
  performance 127–8
  power organizations 130
  profiles 74–5, 78–80
  styles 126–7

teamworking 122–4
teamworking organizations 132–3
learning, transfer 92, 94
Leary, M. 43
Lessem, Ronnie 151, 159, 161, 175
Levinson, Daniel 175
Lievegoed, Bernard 41, 166, 174
literacy, basic 23
Lorenz, K. 148

McDonalds 131
McKinsey and Co 141
Makin, Roger 64
management
  adaptive approach 166–77
  alternative routes to 83–4
  analytical approach 159, 161, 162, 165, 168–9, 171–3
  changing nature 1–2, 69
  identification of potential 110–11, 114–16
  key skills 9, 10
  modes of 10, 43–4, 49–52
  moral and ethical aspects 23–4
  professionalism 23, 26
  styles 113
Management Charter Initiative 4–5
management competency approach 30–1, 34–7
management echelons, British Airways 73–4
management education 4, 147–8
management performance, quality 1–2
management services 167
management teams, action profiling 141–6
managerial portfolio 26
managers
  assessment of performance 14–17
  attributes 9, 10, 11–12, 13–14
  capability to run operations in Africa 118–19
  changing attitudes 101–2
  competence see competence
  criteria for effectiveness 117–18, 119–20
  development 105–6, 152
  entrepreneurial 155
  fundamental activities 42–3, 45–6, 48–9
  self-development 174–5
  specialists versus generalists 81–3
  of Topflight candidates 75–6, 85–6
  in touch with corporate energy 182–3
manufacturing 168
manufacturing company, case study 118–19
market, positioning 152–3
marketing management 164–5
  adaptive 165–6
Marshall, Sir Colin 73
Maslow, Abraham 175

190